Praise for

You Have 4 Minutes to Change Your Life

"I love this book and its approach. It's so easy to think that meditation needs to be difficult and that there's no time to do it, and this book shatters that myth. Whatever challenge you're facing, I know this book contains answers for you, and results you can experience in just a few (4) minutes."

— Nick Ortner, *New York Times* best-selling author of *The Tapping Solution*

"Wow! This isn't just a book. This is a journey. Rebekah's beautiful personal story flows through these pages and I couldn't help but feel so connected to her words like she was taking the words out of my mouth in numerous chapters. This book's inspiring words are truly incredible and I recommend this book to anyone on the path to finding more peace within themselves. In a time when our world is stressed out and chaotic, this book is a beautiful reminder to go within and learn how to love yourself—something I needed many years ago before I started my journey to healing. I wish I had this book 10 years ago to help me navigate life because I've learned that true healing starts within. Thank you, Rebekah, for showing women how to let go, love themselves, and cultivate a radiant relationship with their inner selves. I am buying this book for all the women in my life."

— Amie Valpone, best-selling author of *Eating Clean*

"Rebekah breaks down all the pathways to not simply meditating more, but also shares her busy-mother-of-five-tested practical and doable strategies to actually take the time to connect to yourself in a meaningful and consistent way. From where I stand, the hormonal balance benefits of this kind of doable stress management are game changing. Do this book."

— Alisa Vitti, functional nutritionist, founder of Flo Living and author of *WomanCode*

"I love efficiency and feeling good. This book combines the two beautifully. It's fun and so useful!"

— Kate Northrup, best-selling author of *Money: A Love Story*

"What Rebekah shares in this book is heartfelt, inspiring, and effective. Her simple approach to meditation transcends the noise of spiritual trends and allows the reader to find true connection and healing in a way that works for real life."

— Robyn Youkilis, wellness expert and author of *Go with Your Gut*

"A new, fresh perspective on an ancient practice, Rebekah brings a real-world, tried-and-tested approach to meditation. Hands down, I trust her advice and guidance on how to include meditation in a busy life. Loving, honest, and authentic, this book gives both new and experienced meditators direction on how to make meditation work."

— Alexandra Jamieson, co-creator of *Super Size Me* and author of *Women, Food, and Desire*

FOREWORD

When I first met Rebekah at a Hay House conference in February 2013, I instantly connected with her warmth, authenticity, and positive attitude. Basically, I loved her from day one. She and I are both seekers. We're seekers of health, spiritual wealth, passion, and bliss. These elements contribute to the sweetness in our lives, and if you're like us, you're constantly looking for real ways to squeeze more of them into your busy days. Rebekah and I have studied all aspects of well-being and holistic living for the last decade, and our greatest shared goal is to bring what we've learned to you. We know for sure that one of the best ways to reach your health and wellness goals is through meditation and mindfulness. We believe that meditation can heal your soul and change your life. It's a game changer that can transform your whole world, it costs nothing, and it's 100 percent natural. Meditation is as holistic as it gets. And the best news is that you can experience a fantastic, mind-blowing meditation in 4 minutes or less.

Unfortunately, many people believe meditation is complicated, difficult, time-consuming, or only available to spiritual masters. Absolutely none of that is true. Meditation is for me, it's for Rebekah, and most important, meditation is for you. In Rebekah's extraordinary new book, *You Have 4 Minutes to Change Your Life*, she demystifies meditation and gives you a method you can start practicing immediately. If you have two cheeks to sit on, you can do a great meditation right here, right now. Rebekah breaks down her personal meditation practice into easily understandable steps that are clearly written in plain English. You'll get a little peek at her "woo-woo" side, but you'll also learn practical ways to make meditation your own.

Meditation has helped me overcome many hurdles, including living with a rare form of cancer for well over a decade. As you'll find out in her book, meditation has helped Rebekah, too. She candidly shares her past heartaches and current obstacles through deeply personal stories that will make you feel less alone and more connected. You'll read details about her battles with anxiety and depression and her experiences growing up in poverty and recovering from devastating loss. You'll see that Rebekah knows about pain, stress, and self-destructive behavior, and you'll find so much inspiration in her journey.

Today, Rebekah has transformed herself into a thought leader, TV host, meditation guide, and true friend to thousands of women around the world. She has a strong marriage, five healthy children, a barn full of animals, and a home she loves. But this life she created for herself didn't happen overnight. It took years of self-study, reflection, and healthy habits to turn things around and start moving in a positive, soul-affirming direction. Her daily 4-minute meditation practice, born during her healing journey and the tool she continues to use every single day, is what she's sharing with you in this book. Rebekah is going to show you how to set a brand new course for the rest of your life in just 4 short minutes.

It's no secret that we're stressed out and overwhelmed by the demands of modern life. We're juggling relationships, jobs, family, and bills, and we're putting ourselves last. We feel like we need to say yes to everything even when our gut instincts beg us to say no. It can all feel like too much. When you look at life this way, it's like a heavy suitcase with broken wheels that you have to pick up and carry all by yourself. How do you unpack such big burdens? The answers are in this book. You sit down and take a look at the present moment. You start to notice your breath. You ask yourself, "Am I safe right now? Am I okay right now?" If you're in the present moment, the here and now, the answers will almost always be yes. And if the answer is no, spend 4 minutes with one of Rebekah's meditations.

Rebekah offers many different kinds of meditations for all the situations you face. From overwhelming heartache to struggles with self-esteem, she gives you insightful meditations that cover your most pressing concerns. As a complement to your new practice, she'll also introduce you to hand positions (called mudras) and affirmations (called mantras) that will help you reinforce your positive energy. Of course you know how to breathe, but Rebekah will help you become more aware of your inhales and exhales, allowing you to find your center and to feel more grounded.

Meditation is an essential part of self-care that's proven to reduce stress and quiet your mind. It even strengthens and heals your body. A regular meditation practice fosters happiness and deepens your connection to yourself and others. I have lead meditations for thousands of people, just like Rebekah does on her social media channels. I know about its positive results from what I read in scientific journals, but I also see firsthand how great it is from interacting with people who share their amazing experiences with me.

To sum it up, meditation just works. It's a practical tool that you can use over and over and over again. It's like your home base that's always available and ready for you—whether you're at home, in your car, even in the grocery store. Rebekah's simple practices will help you find more inner calm and peace. They will help you understand yourself more deeply. In just 4 minutes a day, you can live a happier and healthier life, so don't wait another minute to experience that bliss for yourself. If you're ready to feel better, you're in the right place. Just keep reading, dear one.

— Kris Carr, *New York Times* best-selling
author and wellness advocate

Chapter 1

MEDITATION IS EASIER THAN YOU THINK

"I don't have time to meditate."

"Isn't meditation for New Age people or Buddhists?"

"Meditation won't work on serious problems like mine."

These are just a few of the objections I hear from people on a regular basis. If you can't relate to any of these, I'm sure you have a list of your own. If you didn't, you probably wouldn't be reading this book.

Maybe you've tried to meditate before and just gave up. Maybe you don't think you have the patience to meditate or the ability to concentrate. Maybe you're like me, and your life is stressful, allowing you very little time to take care of your own needs.

If any of this sounds familiar, this book is for you.

There's an old Zen proverb that goes like this: "You should sit in meditation for 20 minutes every day—unless you're too busy; then you should sit for an hour."

Don't panic! I did say 4 minutes. I'm not going to make you do *anything* for an hour. I would never ask anything of you that I'm not willing to do myself.

But the truth is that self-care is a must. If you think that taking care of your mental and emotional health is an option that you can ignore because of lack of time, I'm telling you that it's imperative to make it a nonnegotiable—starting now!

I know all too well what it's like. You don't think you have time to take care of yourself, but your life isn't working as well as you'd like. You want more. You want to feel better. You want peace. You want to know how to feel happy in the midst of chaos. You know *something* has to change, but what? Well, that's what *You Have 4 Minutes to Change Your Life* is designed to do for you.

Trust me—I was just like you, and I'm probably still a lot like you. I'm just a regular mom from New Jersey. I've never been to India or worked with a guru in an ashram. But I *have* spent many years studying and teaching yoga and developing specific meditation techniques and mantras that are easy, accessible, and fast. For my life, they had to be! I could do them in 4 minutes—that was it. And consistently devoting just 4 minutes a day to meditation has created dramatic changes in my life. I'm the living proof that this works.

The Day I Discovered Meditation

Just how far have I come? I grew up in a very poor family, and while my parents were loving in many ways, they were dealing with a lot of tough issues. As a result, they fought constantly and neglected my sisters and me. To get attention, I resorted to self-destructive behaviors. I became suicidal. I dropped out of high school, got mixed up in abusive relationships, and became a teen mom.

My family was also deeply religious and involved in an evangelical Christian church, and they looked down on other religions and spiritual traditions. In fact, any traditions that had to do with meditation were downright feared. We believed they were of the devil.

Nevertheless, I'm a naturally curious person, and that fire of curiosity couldn't be put out in me. I was drawn to learning about other traditions, and in the beginning, I thought I was a bad person because of it. Truthfully, I was probably interested in other religions to some degree because it was considered rebellious. While other kids hid drugs or pornography under their mattresses, I hid books about other religions.

When I was 15 years old, my mother worked at a used bookstore that was moving to another location. One afternoon, while helping her pack up the store, I pulled a book off the shelf that had a pretty purple cover with a funny design that I would later learn was a mandala. The book was *Be Here Now* by Ram Dass. I had never seen a book like it before. It was printed on brown craft paper, and the illustrations inside were hand drawn. It was spectacular to me, and even though I couldn't quite articulate why, it excited me.

I knew my mother wouldn't let me read the book if I asked. I knew she would consider it "dangerous." How was I going to get this book? I didn't have the money to buy it, so I did the only thing I felt I could at the time: I stole it. I suppose Ram Dass would forgive me now since the book completely changed my life forever in every way. It became a hidden treasure for me.

I devoured *Be Here Now* again and again. I had no idea what most of it meant, but it still captured my imagination. And I wanted to know more about what Ram Dass talked about, so I made a deep dive into Buddhism, Hinduism, and Eastern thought. I read books like *The Seat of the Soul* by Gary Zukav and *Many Lives, Many Masters* by Dr. Brian Weiss.

I didn't attach a belief system to anything I read at that time, but I was intellectually excited to discover that there were happy people out there practicing something other than Christianity. I had always been told that anything non-Christian was bad. But the people I read about seemed to feel so at peace, and I wanted to feel that, too.

When I read about meditation, it seemed a lot like the prayer practice I'd done my entire life. Instantly I found comfort and excitement in meditation. Prayer had really worked for me, but it had been mostly me asking God for things—favors, a better life, or relief from pain. I begged God to change my external circumstances, the things that were outside of me. Meditation, on the other hand, was a tool for self-examination. Everything happened on the inside. As a teenager, to turn the attention on myself felt indulgent—an indulgence that I relished. Since I wasn't getting a lot of attention from my family, I realized that I could use meditation to pay attention to myself, and feel better in the process.

Making Meditation Work for Me

My meditation practice wasn't regular or disciplined yet. My teenage mind was easily distracted, and I didn't use any particular posture. I didn't even necessarily sit when I did it. There wasn't much privacy in my house, but occasionally I could lock myself in my bedroom and meditate. Sometimes I would meditate on my one-mile walk to or from school. Despite my lack of discipline, there were so many instant rewards for me from meditation. It just goes to show that no matter how much of a beginner you are, and no matter how far from perfect your practice may be, meditation can benefit you immensely.

Of course, the more I learned from books about meditation, the more my practice evolved. But I still resisted a lot of study. What I was doing was working for me, and I didn't want to mess with that. I wanted to see what would happen if I used only the tools I had found inside of me. My education into the way meditation "should" be done was minimal while I established what is now my current practice. So, with little influence, I was able to figure out what works for me. My education since then—learning hand mudras and the Sanskrit names for meditation postures (you'll learn about these in the next chapter)—has only validated the "realness" of my practice. I was able to build it based on what feels good rather than what's "supposed" to work, and you can do the same.

The result of this self-teaching approach has been amazing for me. In spite of my very difficult beginnings, I now have a beautiful marriage, five gorgeous children, and a great career. In my work I can express myself freely every day, wholeheartedly connect with people, and live my life with passion and purpose. That work led me to found my own wellness movement, become a fitness and yoga instructor, teach meditation on my own TV show, and create my 4-minute meditation videos on YouTube for people all over the world. This is what happens when you share wonderful, life-changing discoveries with the world. You give back in service, and the Universe blesses you with even more good fortune to spread around.

When I was a child, I mostly hated my life. Today I love my life. It perks me up better than coffee. The sheer possibilities in every day compel me to jump out of bed in the morning—no caffeine required. Meditation lights up my life.

I'm not bragging. I'm telling you this to show you that a simple practice of 4-minute meditations every day can make all the difference in your life. Yes, there's work to be done in order to heal. I'm not claiming that everything in your entire life will be different on the very first day of your new practice. But in time, sitting for those 4 minutes a day on a consistent basis will help you change your behaviors and open your heart to yourself and others. The results can be miraculous.

If I can do it, you absolutely can, too. There's nothing special or unique about me that isn't equally special or unique about you. We have all been given the tools to create our own happiness.

When I was a kid, I never dreamed that I would have the life I have today. It didn't feel possible. Today I'm so removed from the person I was when I was younger that when I talk about her, it almost feels like I'm talking about someone else. That's how much you can grow and change if you commit to just those 4 minutes daily.

How to Use This Book

In Chapter 2, I'll give you meditation tips and tools to help you get started. These will include:

- Postures – Different ways to sit during meditation that will help you stay alert and comfortable. Find one that works for you!

- Breath – Patterns to help focus your meditation. I'll show you how to practice a few simple techniques.

- Mantras – Repeated words, phrases, or sounds used to quiet outside distractions and eliminate unwanted thoughts.

- Mudras – Finger/hand positions that might help you access certain emotions or bring ease to physical and emotional struggles.

- Props – Items that could aid in proper physical alignment and help you feel more comfortable in your postures.

- Chakras – A brief primer on the seven energetic centers in your body. Working with chakras might help you open up more—physically and emotionally.

- Finding Time to Meditate – I'll show you that even if your life is busy and chaotic, you can still find time for a meditation practice.

After reading these tips, you'll feel more confident about your new practice and will erase the needless "mystery" surrounding meditation. Try the different methods and discover what works for you. Then you can throw out the rest. There's no right or wrong way to meditate; all that counts is that you find a way to do it that serves you best.

The last section of Chapter 2 is called "Meditation Isn't for Me Because . . ." and includes the most common questions and objections that I've crowd-sourced from my followers. These include:

- Is it OK to lie down during meditation?
- Do I have to have total silence to meditate?
- Do my eyes have to stay closed during meditation?
- What do I do if my body starts to hurt?

Once you've explored the basics in Chapter 2, you're ready for Chapters 3 through 11, which are the "magic nine"—nine issues that we all face in our lives. These chapters include ways that meditation can help you through the hard times, as well as help you transform from within so that (1) you'll learn how to handle life's challenges better and (2) your life will actually *get* better.

Each of the chapters includes a story from my life that shows how meditation has helped me overcome some pretty hefty challenges throughout the years. Some of the stories are funny and light, and others are pretty heavy. I've never shared some of these stories with anyone, but I'm excited to share them with you in the hope that the lessons I've learned can help you in your own life.

Each chapter also includes "Spread the Love" affirmations that you can share with your friends and followers on social media. Copy the affirmation in a tweet or Facebook post, or take a pic to share on Instagram or Snapchat, and use the hashtag #YH4M.

Of course, the cornerstone of each of the nine chapters is the mantra and 4-minute meditation. These mantras and meditations have helped me deal with stress, low self-esteem, anxiety, body issues, grief, emotional and physical wounds, and relationship problems. They have also helped me cultivate courage, confidence, gratitude, abundance, success, and true happiness. These tools have changed my life! And I believe they can do the same for you.

Most importantly they're easy, accessible, and transformative. Meditation doesn't have to be difficult. Don't get me wrong: deep-diving into your psyche is important work. But there's also a lot of happiness and peace that you can harness right here, right now at the surface, and these 4-minute meditations will help you do that. There is sweetness in the simple and scrumptiousness in the uncomplicated.

Peace, calm, happiness—whatever you desire is already being set in motion. You can make your life amazing without ever attending an expensive workshop or visiting an ashram or dedicating hours of your week to it. You're ready for it; it's waiting for you.

I hope that after you've read the book, you'll keep it by your favorite meditation spot for reference—like a meditation toolkit—for years to come. You can use the mantras and meditations in the chapters over and over again, as needed. By the last chapter, you'll be someone who can meditate comfortably, regularly, and effectively—even if you thought you would never be able to meditate.

Changing your outlook and your whole life is easier than you ever thought—I promise! Turn the page, and let me show you just how simple it can be. Let's approach life with *ease* today and see what happens.

> *"When you change the way you look at things, the things you look at change."*
>
> — Dr. Wayne W. Dyer

Chapter 2

GETTING STARTED—
MEDITATION *YOUR* WAY

"Yes, I see you. I recognize that you're a thinking, feeling person, and I'm here to listen." That's the essence and magic of meditation—the gift of telling yourself that you matter and that you're worth time and attention. No pomp. No circumstance. No rules. Just showing up for yourself with compassion and without judgment. When this is your practice, meditation can serve as a mirror and the lighthouse that leads you home.

That's probably not going to be what you find when you type "meditation" into your browser's search bar, but after all my years of reading, researching, and practicing, this is the most accurate definition of meditation that I can come up with. At least it's the most truthful as it relates to my personal practice. Meditation allows me to be a close friend and ally to myself, while also placing me in the role of objective observer. It's like those magnifying beauty mirrors that show all your pores—like, *each* one of them. Meditation magnifies and focuses attention on the parts of us that so desperately need attention but often are ignored. When practiced consistently, meditation is an efficient, no-frills, and practical means of discovery and self-healing.

So, why isn't every person on the planet practicing meditation on a daily basis? Like every other great Universal truth—which are all super simple messages when broken down—meditation has been plagued by mystery and misconceptions. The practice of meditation has also been overcomplicated by some who would have you believe there's only one way to meditate—their way. Well, I believe meditation is for everyone, and there are as many effective ways to do it as there are people on this planet.

You aren't going to find a lot of esoteric, head-in-the-clouds talk in this book . . . OK, maybe just a *little*. But I want to meet you exactly where you are, and at least for now, that's down here on earth.

Later in this chapter, there's a list of the most popular questions I get about meditation from my followers, but right now, I'd like to go over the three most common meditation myths that I've noticed over the years.

Myth #1. Meditation is about not thinking about anything. If the only way to meditate successfully was to clear your mind of all thoughts, no one would meditate—ever. Not thinking about anything is virtually impossible! While a totally silent mind is a great goal to look forward to after years (if not a lifetime) of regular practice, it's important to know that you can experience the benefits of meditation the very first time you sit down, close your eyes, and take ten deep breaths. Meditation is for everyone at every level of experience. Instead of trying to empty your mind of all thoughts, try focusing on just one thought, and simply observe what happens.

Myth #2. You have to meditate for long periods of time. Are you forcing yourself to meditate longer than what feels comfortable? The benefits of meditation come from the *quality* of your time on your pillow, not the *quantity* of time. We live in a busy world, and there are many more responsibilities and requirements thrust upon us every day. Stressing out over whether or not you're spending enough time in meditation is a worry you don't need to take on. Are you able to find a quiet place where you can sit undisturbed for just a few minutes? Is it possible for you to close your eyes for just a few deep breaths? Can you sit comfortably in a relaxed position long enough to release some tension from your muscles? Those are the qualities of a good meditation practice. In time or at different times, you'll be able to carve out more minutes for your practice. But if all you have is 4 minutes to spare, that's perfectly fine.

Myth #3. Meditation is about spirituality. Meditation is actually a practical tool for managing stress and maintaining balance. It doesn't belong to any religion or specific philosophy. While many people use meditation as part of their religious practices, there's no requirement to be spiritual or believe in a higher power. Meditation has been used for centuries as a means of maintaining mental, emotional, and physical health. Don't knock it because you don't consider yourself to be a spiritual person. Science has supported the benefits of meditation for ages, and it can be a practical and powerful tool in helping you reach your goals.

Doesn't reading that make you feel better already?

I know that whenever I attempt something new, I always have a little anxiety about messing up—especially if I'm doing it in front of other people or if I have a lot riding on the outcome. If you're suffering from stress and turning to meditation to ease that stress, the last thing you need is to generate new stress about whether you're doing it right.

I assure you there's virtually no way to fail at meditation. If you're taking the time to get quiet, be still, and follow your breath, you're 90 percent of the way to a completely successful meditation practice. Even better, lasting and profound change can be achieved in just the consistent *effort* to practice meditation. How exciting is that?

Now that we've established that meditation doesn't have to be hard, that it doesn't have to take a lot of time, and that you don't have to be a spiritual being on the fast track to enlightenment, let me give you the basics and how you can create a practice that suits your life—as it is today. I want to guide you toward a practice of meditation *your* way, and that means using the skills and tools that you already possess.

Each chapter's meditations begin with a "preparation" section, where you'll find directions on which position—or posture—that I feel best complements that particular meditation. Postures need to serve you during your practice, and they won't serve you if the position is uncomfortable for you. Pain is an indication that something is wrong, so don't sacrifice your well-being for a "perfect" posture.

You may find, however, that the more you practice, the easier a once-awkward posture becomes. Continue to check in with yourself to see if you're experiencing only minor discomfort or true pain. Some discomfort can be normal (as long as it doesn't hinder your ability to relax and concentrate), but pain must never be tolerated.

I encourage you to try all the poses in this chapter. If you find that the recommended posture distracts from your practice, feel free to substitute another posture that's more comfortable for you.

I will also discuss the use of basic props that can provide increased comfort and support, and help you maintain proper physical alignment. Don't worry about buying expensive equipment, though. Almost any fancy meditation prop can be replicated easily with normal household items, such as blankets and pillows.

Now, you don't have to read this chapter all the way through, although you might like to read the Q&A at the end. This chapter is for reference to help you do the meditations in each of the chapters that follow. So, read a little, read a lot, or skip ahead to whatever chapter calls you most. Remember: It's meditation *your way*. Before you try your first meditation, however, please come back and read through the basics in this chapter. You'll feel a lot more comfortable with your meditations if you do. Then you can refer back to it whenever you need a refresher.

Meditation Postures Anyone Can Do

If you're just beginning a meditation practice but have practiced yoga in the past, you may already be familiar with many of the postures in this chapter. But even if you've never taken a yoga class, I'm sure you'll be able to achieve a comfortable meditation posture just by following a few easy cues.

Easy Seat / Sukhasana

Most of the meditations in this book will require you to sit in your *Easy* or *Comfortable* Seat—*Sukhasana* in Sanskrit. If you have ever sat in a circle on the floor in school, you already know the basics of this posture. You've been doing it since kindergarten.

Easy Seat can be practiced anywhere you feel comfortable and supported. I practice on a buckwheat-filled lotus pillow (like the one in the illustration) on the floor, but you can sit on the couch, on your bed, or wherever you can sit up straight with enough space to cross your legs. Sitting on a pillow is recommended because it allows for proper physical alignment of the spine and hips. If you don't have a firm pillow, you can also fold a thick blanket until it's 4 to 6 inches high.

How to Get into Easy Seat

1. Sit on the front edge of your pillow or blanket, allowing your legs to stretch out in front of you.

2. Cross one leg over the other at your ankles.

3. Draw your knees outward as you move them closer to your torso. As your knees draw toward your torso, each foot will find its way under the opposite knee.

4. There should be space between your pelvis and your shins, and there should be no feeling of strain in this position. If having your legs crossed is uncomfortable, place one foot (or shin) in front of the other with the outer edge of each foot resting comfortably on the floor.

5. Sitting up tall, imagine your vertebrae stacked one on top of the other.

6. With a big inhale, lift your shoulders up toward your ears. On exhale, roll your shoulder blades back and down along your spine. This will leave your shoulders broad and your chest open.

7. Now imagine that a string is attached to the crown of your head, pulling your head toward the sky. Make sure that your chin is parallel to the floor and not tucked down or tilted upward.

8. Your hands can rest on your thighs or knees with palms down, or you can turn your palms upward during meditations to energize you.

Hero Pose / Virasana

This seated pose is a great alternative to the cross-legged Easy Seat. Hero Pose (*Virasana* in Sanskrit) can be performed with your bottom directly on the floor or seated on a pillow, block, blanket, or bolster. This pose perfectly complements meditations for cultivating increased energy. It's called the *hero* pose because you'll feel strong and energized when in this posture.

How to Get into Hero Pose

1. Kneel on the floor with your knees touching. You might want to place a block, bolster, or rolled blanket in between your calves before you attempt this pose for the first time.

2. Spread your legs until they're slightly wider than hip's width apart. The tops of your feet should lie flat on the floor.

3. Lower your seat until you're resting firmly on your prop or the floor (allow for about a one-inch gap

between the inner edge of each foot and the outer edges of each hip).

4.   Inhale your shoulders up to your ears. Then exhale your shoulder blades back and down along your spine. Your front shoulders and chest will be open wide, and you will be sitting up nice and straight like a triumphant hero.

Semireclined Bound Angle Pose / Supta Baddha Konasana

A few meditations are better practiced in a supported position. Semireclined Bound Angle Pose, also known in Sanskrit as *Supta Baddha Konasana*, allows you to feel relaxed and supported while also opening your hips and chest. The hip joints and chest are two points on the body that, when allowed to be more open, can provide tremendous emotional release. It's always good to stay vulnerable during meditation, and positioning yourself in a posture that can help to access a vulnerable state more easily will allow you to reap the benefits of certain meditations.

The true expression of Supta Baddha Konasana would have you reclined all the way, lying flat on the floor. But one of my few meditation rules—though none of them is law—is that it's better if you aren't lying down. (I'll get into why in the Q&A section on page 34.)

There are times, however, when I'll suggest Corpse Pose (*Savasana* in Sanskrit) as an alternative pose. Corpse Pose is performed simply by lying down on your back with your arms outstretched, palms facing up or turned down, with your hands and feet relaxed. I may also suggest that you bend your knees and place the soles of your feet flat on the floor.

But let's concentrate for now on the Semireclined Bound Angle Pose.

How to Get into Semireclined Bound Angle Pose

1. Find a firm, flat surface where you can sit comfortably for an extended period of time. You'll be in the pose for the duration of your meditation. Place a blanket or yoga mat underneath you for extra padding.

2. Place a stack of firm pillows, cushions, or a bolster lengthwise up and down your spine. Make sure you're completely supported without straining to stay upright. I recommend that you create an angle no less than 45 degrees between your back and the floor.

3. Bend your knees, and place the inner edges of your feet together.

4. Slowly drop your knees open toward the floor. Resist any urge to hyperextend your hips by pushing your knees closer to the floor. (It may feel good to support your knees with blocks if they don't reach the floor.)

5. At this time, the soles of your feet should be touching. Feel free to position your feet closer to or farther from your hips.

6. Last, allow your arms to fall to your sides with your palms upturned.

Chair Meditation Pose

Sitting on the floor or crossing your legs might be uncomfortable or even painful for you. If so, don't worry. You can meditate anywhere, including on a chair. Your seat at the breakfast table may turn out to be your favorite place to meditate before you start your day. Or maybe you have a stressful desk job, and you'd like to take short breaks throughout the day to check in and re-center. A chair meditation can be the perfect (and inconspicuous) way to fit a little self-care into a hectic day.

This seated posture may be the easiest, most convenient meditation pose you'll ever do, so be prepared to love it and use it all the time.

How to Get into Chair Meditation Pose

1. Find a chair that allows for your knees and hips to be at approximately the same height.

2. Sit up tall and press your back firmly against the back of the chair or in a way that allows for an imaginary

straight line to be drawn from the crown of your head, down your back, and to your seat.

3. Your knees should be about hip's width apart (or a little wider) and your ankles should be directly under your knees.

4. Make sure your feet are placed firmly and completely on the floor.

5. You can rest your hands on your knees or thighs with your palms upturned, facing down, or in your choice of hand mudra. (Look for an explanation of basic hand mudras later in this chapter on pages 25–29.)

Basic Props to Complement Your Postures

I'm not going to give you a giant shopping list of expensive accessories that will only end up in your fitness equipment graveyard. (Remember the ThighMaster?) But sometimes sitting on the floor can be uncomfortable, and your level of comfort in any pose can change from day to day. Props not only allow for increased comfort in a pose but they can also provide for better alignment and, therefore, the more correct expression of a pose.

The following are props that I keep in my personal collection and recommend that you keep in your meditation "toolbox" as well. You can find most of these props at a local sports store or any big-box store with a fitness department. There are also countless online sites that offer yoga accessories at a discount. You'll notice that most of the props serve a similar purpose, so you may discover that you like using only one or two from the list. The good news is that they're all relatively inexpensive, so there's very little risk of buyer's remorse. (I'm reminded of the $2,000 treadmill / coat rack in my basement.)

- Block – A dense foam or cork block useful in seated positions to elevate your seat or to support your back, head, or knees in reclined positions. Use with Easy Seat, Hero Pose, and Semireclined Bound Angle Pose.

- Bolster or Pillow – A firm pillow filled with cotton stuffing or buckwheat, useful in both seated and reclined positions to elevate your seat, back, head, or neck. Use with Easy Seat, Hero Pose, and Semireclined Bound Angle Pose.

- Traditional Mexican Yoga Blanket – Unfold to use as a mat in reclined poses, roll to use as a head or neck pillow, or fold to use in place of a block or bolster in seated poses. Use with Easy Seat, Hero Pose, Semireclined Bound Angle Pose, and Corpse Pose.

- Yoga Mat – Unroll to create a softer floor surface for seated or reclined positions, or roll to use as head or neck support. Use with Easy Seat, Hero Pose, Semireclined Bound Angle Pose, and Corpse Pose. (Least recommended because it's harder to manipulate and not made for support, but something that you may already own.)

- Meditation Kneeling Chair – Useful for relieving strain, increasing circulation, and supporting better alignment in Hero Pose. (This is the priciest option. Use in kneeling positions as an upgrade from your block, bolster, pillow, or blanket.)

If You Can Breathe, You Can Meditate

Tirumalai Krishnamacharya, an Indian yoga teacher who is revered by many as one of the most influential figures in modern yoga, was known to say, "If you can breathe, you can do yoga." This is not to say that he didn't believe in the importance of a practice based on careful study, discipline, and consistency. But his beliefs that yoga is for everyone and that it starts with the breath are core principles that I also apply to meditation. If you can breathe, you can meditate.

To practice the meditations in this book, you'll need to learn only three simple breathing techniques: Easy Breath, Even Breath, and One-Two Breath. Easy Breath simply requires you to focus your attention on your breath so that you can follow its path through your body. During other meditations, I'll recommend that you practice an Even Breath or a One-Two Breath. These last two breathing methods are particularly useful for easing anxiety.

Easy Breath

This technique is basically the breathing version of Easy Seat. It requires only that you focus your attention on your natural inhales and exhales as they are in the moment that you begin your meditation. No counting and no pressure to make your breaths deep or long. You just focus your attention on whatever is happening in the present moment.

One of my favorite "laws of the Universe" states that the simple act of observation changes what's being observed. I won't pretend to be a scientist, but I can tell you that every time I've observed my own breath or instructed a student to do so, the breath changes on its own—and always in a positive way. Through the simple act of observation, the breath becomes smoother, longer, and deeper, without any effort at all. It's an experiment I've conducted at least a thousand times with 100 percent good results.

How to Practice Easy Breath

1. Follow the path of your breath in through your nose and down the back of your throat.

2. Feel your lungs fill with air before your breath enters your belly.

3. Allow your belly to feel loose as it expands and fills with your breath.

4. Take a moment as your breath settles into your seat before you allow it to turn and exit your body, feeling your belly and your lungs contract, and then noticing how your breath is warmer as it makes its way up through your throat and past your lips.

Even Breath

Even Breath is exactly what it sounds like. Each inhale should fill your body completely, and each exhale should empty all the air out of your body while matching the duration of the inhalation. Your Even Breath should be smooth, measured, and relaxed, but also intentional and focused. It may help to count silently to yourself to make sure each inhale and exhale match in duration.

How to Practice Even Breath

1. Inhale through your nose, mimicking the pattern of your Easy Breath.

2. Exhale through your mouth while allowing your jaw to relax. Focus on letting every bit of air escape your body.

3. Pause for one beat before beginning your next breath cycle.

One-Two Breath

This is my favorite breathing technique for cultivating a state of peace and calm, especially when I find myself feeling anxious, panicked, or afraid. When practicing meditation as a means to relieve stress or anxiety, distracting the mind from racing thoughts becomes the main focus. You can shift your thoughts away from the negative and toward something safe and neutral by paying careful attention to the breath cycle.

The One-Two Breath method requires greater focus and control than the other breathing techniques I've mentioned, so it's more effective for occupying your mind and shifting thought processes.

How to Practice One-Two Breath

1. Inhale through your nose, mimicking the pattern of your Easy Breath, while counting the seconds of your inhalation silently.

2. Exhale slowly through your mouth, doubling the duration on your inhale. For example, if you count to three during your inhale, make sure your exhale extends for a full six counts.

3. Pause for as long as it feels comfortable at the bottom of every breath cycle. By allowing yourself to rest in emptiness, you create space in both your mind and body.

Make Your Words (and Thoughts) Count

I just explained how focusing on your breath can distract you from thoughts that aren't serving you. Mantras—words, phrases, or sounds that are repeated to aid concentration in meditation— also provide protection from a busy mind. The word "mantra" is a combination of two Sanskrit words: "man" (mind) and "tra" (instrument). I use mantras in nearly all my guided meditations to not only drown out the negative noise and mental chitchat (known as *chitta vritti* in Sanskrit) but also to introduce new positive thoughts.

Words are incredibly powerful, and the messages we hear on a constant basis—from others or in our own thoughts—shape our subconscious and influence the way we feel, speak, and behave. Repeating mantras and positive affirmations during my meditations allows me to create new conversations with myself around situations that may be causing unease in my life.

Imagine for a moment how amazing it would feel to hear only positive, uplifting words about your body. Compliments come from every direction, as friends, family, and co-workers tell you how great you look every chance they get. What if those same conversations were happening inside your head? Negative self-speak no longer exists. How would hearing only good things about your body change the way you feel, speak, and behave? Would you feel more confident, outgoing, and assertive? How would your new attitude and behaviors serve you? Maybe goals would feel less out of reach, and you'd meet new opportunities with excitement instead of fear.

You can choose to fill your mental space with any thoughts you'd like, but the space is limited. There's room for only one thought and one action at a time. When you choose to be still in meditation and think of something positive, you edge out everything else that doesn't serve you. One breath at a time, one thought at a time, and one mantra at a time takes you closer and closer to peace, calm, and happiness.

Using Hand Mudras

Mudras, symbolic or ritual gestures with origins in Hinduism and Buddhism, are believed to influence the way energy flows through the body. From the Sanskrit word for *sign* or *seal*, a mudra may involve different parts of the body or the whole body. There are also myriad variations of mudras using only the hands. For the purpose of keeping it simple, I'm going to offer my favorite hand mudras with easy instructions on how to perform each. You might enjoy giving them a try.

I'm sure you've seen one or more of these mudras before. Statues of the Buddha and Hindu deities often show the figures with their hands placed in mudra positions. Other religions use hand mudras as well. One of the most popular and easily recognizable hand mudras in the Western world is the simple Anjali Mudra, which looks identical to holding the hands together as if in prayer. Pressing the palms and outstretched fingers together is believed to bring energies into balance and to center the practitioner. I use the Anjali Mudra with the tips of my thumbs pressed against my heart center (or sternum) during meditations for gratitude or surrender.

According to the ancient traditions of Buddhism and Hinduism, the body is composed of the same five elements as the Universe and represented by each finger:

- Thumb – Fire
- Index Finger – Air
- Middle Finger – Space
- Ring Finger – Earth
- Pinkie Finger – Water

A quick Google search for "hand mudras" will lead you to many excellent resources that outline how to use mudras for any condition, mood, or ailment you wish to treat. I haven't personally experimented with mudras to treat health conditions, but I do pay careful attention to my hand positions during every meditation. It also may be interesting to observe your own hands during meditation to see what feels most comfortable and natural for you.

When you pay attention to your hands during meditation or throughout the day, you might discover that you use different movements and positions to express yourself without even realizing it. One position a lot of people use unconsciously in everyday life is touching the tips of their fingers on one hand to the corresponding fingers of the other hand. This position aids in concentration and is used most often while explaining something important.

In addition to the hand positions I mentioned above, I've handpicked the following mudras for you to use with the meditations in this book. Refer back to the description for each hand mudra when you encounter them in the meditation instructions.

- Gyan Mudra – Connect the tips of your index finger and thumb. Allow the other fingers to remain outstretched without becoming stiff. This mudra is indicated for grounding, calming, improving concentration, and stimulating wisdom and knowledge.

- Surya Mudra – Place the tip of your bent ring finger at the inside base of your thumb. Gently press your thumb over the top of your bent ring finger. Surya Mudra has been used to increase body temperature, as an aid in digestion, and for weight loss support.

- Kubera Mudra – Also known as the prosperity mudra, Kubera Mudra is done by placing the tips of your bent ring and pinkie fingers on the middle of your palm while connecting the tips of your thumb, index, and middle fingers. Use this mudra for meditations on abundance, wealth, and confidence.

- Cup/Chalice Mudra – Perform this two-handed mudra by cradling your left hand with your right (palms facing up) and connecting the tips of both thumbs. Both hands should rest on  your lap. If you're sitting with your legs crossed, the hand on top should correspond with the leg that's on top. (In other words, if your right leg is crossed over your left, place your right hand inside your left hand.) Use this mudra to balance energy in your body.

- Palms Up / Palms Down – For most meditations, I recommend that you place your hands on your knees or thighs with your palms facing either up or down. The simple act of turning your palms upward invites energy from the space around you. Placing your palms down offers protection and seals your energy during your practice.

Chakras: The Spinning Wheels Inside Your Body

The word *chakra* is derived from the Sanskrit word for *wheel* or *circle*. There are many different chakra systems in Eastern traditions, but most Westerners observe a common system that names seven major chakras, or energy centers, in the body.

Chakras are believed to be a part of a system of invisible, energetic passageways (nadis) that allow life force (prana) to travel through your body. A clear and spinning chakra is a healthy chakra. It means that energy is moving along as it should, and all is well. A blocked or slow-moving chakra can cause some real trouble energetically and physically. For instance, if your Throat Chakra gets a little clogged (like, maybe you have a frog stuck in your throat), you might have trouble communicating or expressing your feelings. There have been many times in my life that I've felt stuck, and a good chakra clearing fixed me right up.

How do you clear a chakra? There are countless techniques for connecting with your chakras and getting them spinning again. Just focusing on a particular chakra and giving it some extra love and attention will charge it up. Some of the meditations in this book will also help you balance your chakras.

Each chakra is assigned a color, function, and location in the physical body. Refer to the below list of the seven major chakras and their colors, locations, and functions.

1. Root Chakra

    -   Color: red
    -   Location: groin area, pelvic floor, and the base of the spine (the body's base)
    -   Function: represents foundation, security, survival, the feeling of being grounded

2. Sacral Chakra

    -   Color: orange
    -   Location: lower abdomen
    -   Function: represents sexual energy, creativity, well-being, pleasure

3. Solar Plexus Chakra
   - Color: yellow
   - Location: stomach or gut
   - Function: personal power, self-esteem, confidence, mental energy

4. Heart Chakra
   - Color: green
   - Location: heart/chest
   - Function: love, compassion, empathy, joy

5. Throat Chakra
   - Color: blue
   - Location: throat
   - Function: communication, self-expression, speech, truthfulness

6. Third Eye Chakra
   - Color: indigo
   - Location: between the eyebrows
   - Function: intuition, imagination, wisdom, psychic abilities

7. Crown Chakra
   - Color: violet
   - Location: top of the head
   - Function: connection to the Divine, spirituality

I don't often include chakras as part of my practice, but I've experienced some great results from simply having a general understanding of what they are and how they're supposed to work. I know you may be skeptical about things like invisible energetic wheels that spin inside and within the energy field outside your body, but if you keep your mind and heart open to the possibility that they're real, you may experience some exciting shifts that have you busting through emotional blocks in no time. You never know until you try!

You Have 4 Minutes to Meditate

If I had a nickel for every time someone told me they don't have enough time to meditate, I'd be writing this book from the patio of my Tuscan villa and not my screened porch in New Jersey. I know your life is busy. I know you feel like you barely have time to even *read* your to-do list some days let alone check anything off. But I also know that when you take a little time to get centered, check in with yourself, and make yourself feel like you're worthy of a little loving attention, everything that used to get you frazzled is suddenly more tolerable.

Meditation helps sort stuff out. It's like an emotional closet organizer. Any stressful issues you've stuffed, piled, or hidden in your closet will get placed neatly in their proper spots during meditation. The time you spend on your pillow (or wherever you choose to meditate) provides an opportunity for you to see your issues more clearly, and this allows you to deal with these issues without becoming overwhelmed.

One good meditation won't keep your closet clean forever, of course. Your emotional closet will become untidy again from time to time. After all, you can't vacuum the floor once in your life and say, "That's done." This is why a consistent meditation practice is important. Each time you return to your pillow, the process will be a little easier. Rather than having a giant pile of mess to deal with, you'll only have to remind yourself where your "stuff" goes and put it back in its place. Do you see where I'm going with this? Tidying just takes a few minutes if you're only picking up a couple of things at a time and you know where everything goes. It takes a lot longer if you've let stuff pile up for a while.

Over time, your stress level will start to shrink and whatever issues you're dealing with will become less overwhelming, simply because you're taking just a little bit of time every day to tidy your emotional clutter.

Meditation doesn't have to take a long time to be effective. If that were true, I wouldn't have a meditation practice at all. My meditations are short because *my* life is busy. (I have five kids, remember?) I created a practice that fits my life because I don't have the time to create a life that fits a practice. You can use my meditations at any time and in any place you choose. They're made to fit into *your* busy schedule.

Four minutes is about the same time it takes to sit through a commercial break of *The Real Housewives* (my favorite non-guilty pleasure). Imagine taking a few minutes to re-center yourself instead of fast-forwarding through the commercials the next time you watch your favorite show on the DVR. Or imagine the next time you go out for groceries, you take 4 minutes in the parking lot to check in with how you're feeling instead of bolting out of your car and into the chaos of the store. It's really that easy to make time for yourself. And when you do take time, you'll be amazed at how a little investment can deliver such profound and life-changing rewards.

Now that I've convinced you that you do, in fact, have lots of opportunities to meditate, let's handle those other worries and objections.

"Meditation Isn't for Me Because . . ."

When I put out a request for questions about meditation from my social media followers, I was shocked at how many responses I got. The answers not only revealed that there's a lot of confusion about what meditation is and why people should do it, but there's a lot of fear attached to meditation, too. People are afraid to even try it. I chalk this up to two main reasons:

- Meditation is still considered to be a strange "alternative" to conventional health and wellness practices, and, therefore, it's shrouded in mystery.

- There are too many "gurus" giving giant lists of right and wrong ways to meditate.

I've gathered the most common questions and objections I received and put together a list with answers. My answers are only suggestions that you can apply to your own practice as you see fit.

Meditation Q&A

Q: Is it OK to lie down during meditation?

A: The main purpose of meditation is to focus your attention, not to relax. The relaxation happens because your mind becomes more settled. In most cases, there's no need to place your body in a physically relaxed position, but I do understand why that would be appealing.

The ideal position for meditation is one that allows you to stay upright, focused, and alert without discomfort, providing a clear path for energy to flow through your body (no slumping or bending over). If you want to feel physically comfortable, choose a posture that allows you to be supported, but not one that has you lying down completely flat. Becoming so relaxed that you fall asleep during meditation isn't ideal (unless you're practicing meditation for insomnia).

Q: Do I have to have total silence to meditate?

A: I would love to have a perfectly quiet space for my meditation practice, but that isn't my reality. Whether it's the sounds of my five kids clomping up and down stairs and playing their instruments, or the noise of traffic when I'm parked in my car, I'm constantly surrounded by noise.

Most of us live in less-than-peaceful environments, so it's probably a good idea to accept that a silent meditation space isn't always a realistic goal. And that's OK. Your meditation practice should meet you where you are, noise and all. If you can't secure a completely silent space for your practice, try to find a space that offers the *most* amount of quiet. Then, instead of letting the noise distract you, say to yourself, "All the noise in my current environment is here in service of my practice. It teaches me how to navigate through every day with ease."

And if you do have a perfectly quiet place to meditate, awesome! Can I come over?

Q: Do my eyes have to stay closed during meditation?

A: No. There are actually types of meditation—candle-gazing, for instance—that require you to keep your eyes open. However, closing your eyes during meditation has the obvious benefit of removing visual distractions, so I recommend keeping your eyes closed simply because it will be easier for you to concentrate.

What I didn't realize until recently, though, is that some people feel uncomfortable—even unsafe—with their eyes closed. Not being able to see makes some people feel vulnerable, and that could trigger a past trauma, making concentration impossible. If this is the case for you, don't worry. You can practice meditation with your eyes open and still reap plenty of benefits. If you're concerned that you won't be able to concentrate, try gazing at a candle flame or another favorite object. It's important to focus your eyes softly on whatever you choose. Avoid giving yourself a headache or eye strain.

Q: What do I do if my body starts to hurt?

A: Never tolerate pain during meditation. It's normal to feel uncomfortable for a few moments, especially when trying a new pose, but if your body starts to hurt, move. You may become unfocused for a moment, but that's far better than struggling through an entire meditation in pain.

Q: Is it normal to cry during or after meditation?

A: This is one of the most frequent questions I get about meditation. It usually comes to me by way of private message because people feel self-conscious about it. If you've cried during meditation, know that you're not alone. People cry in meditation all the time.

Crying is also common in yoga class. When new muscle groups are stretched, or an opening happens (for a lot of women, it's all about the hips), the energy release may come with tears. Our emotional and physical selves are tethered. Feelings don't live just in the mind; they take root in the physical body as well. Have you ever had a stress headache or pain in your chest from heartbreak? That's your body reacting to emotional pain. Have you ever had a sudden burst of energy or an overall feeling of wellness when you hear good news? It's all connected!

Similarly, if you remove mental distractions and uncover underlying issues and feelings during meditation, you may experience a physical reaction. This reaction can sometimes take the form of a little bit (or even a lot) of crying. Bottom line: it's normal.

Emotional openings are so important to the evolution of our spirit, so don't try to avoid them. We hide and bury our feelings constantly for the sake of self-preservation. It's a survival technique built into our DNA.

Meditation allows us to transcend the trappings of our humanness, open doors to hidden emotions, and get in touch with God and our own spiritual selves.

If you start to feel overwhelmed with emotion during meditation, remind yourself that you're in a safe place and that no physical harm can come to you. You may want to repeat, "I am safe. I am calm. I choose to be here," on each exhale until the feeling has passed.

Q: How do I know which type of meditation is best for me?

A: I get it. You want the best. You want to know exactly what works and how it's going to work for you so that you can enjoy the best possible outcome. I can easily replace "meditation" for "diet" or "exercise" in your question and still end up giving you the same response: the best thing for you is the thing you'll actually do.

You could ask me, "Is Transcendental Meditation the best meditation for me?" And I'd respond, "Is it working for you?" If the answer is "yes," then it's the best meditation for you. Transcendental Meditation works; hundreds of legitimate studies have proven its effectiveness. But I also know that sitting still for 15 to 20 minutes sounds like torture to a lot of people. For those people, a shorter meditation or a moving meditation may serve them better.

There's a good, better, and best for anything that helps you live a fuller life. While we'd all like to do the best for ourselves, the best that exists in a vacuum or a scientific study isn't always going to be the best at fitting into our lives. I don't eat a 100 percent organic, sustainably grown, locally sourced diet of only foods harvested in season. Still, my diet is pretty awesome, and it serves me well, even though it's never going to be "perfect."

Throughout this book, I'll offer you lots of different choices for your meditation practice. It's your job to try them out and decide which tools actually help you build *your* version of a happy life. Take one, or grab them all. Dig around inside, show up to work with your new tools, and I promise that you'll be pleased with your payday.

Chapter 3

4 Minutes to De-Stress Your Life

I readily admit that I'm a person who lives with stress and anxiety . . . but I don't *suffer* from stress and anxiety. How is that possible? Someone who *suffers* from stress and/or anxiety has yet to learn how to deal with them as part of daily life. Someone who *lives* with stress and anxiety has learned how to function with them so that they don't cause so much suffering. Today, after having built "muscle" for managing the stress and anxiety in my life, I've been able to help others do the same. If you suffer from stress and anxiety—no matter how severe—you *can* significantly reduce the suffering.

But don't mistake *managing* stress with *curing* it. When we make it our mission to cure ourselves of our anxieties, we become stressed about being stressed. We become anxious about feeling anxious. It's a double whammy that often leads to self-judgment. "I'm still feeling anxious. What's wrong with me?" "I must not be meditating the right way or I wouldn't still have this stress in my life." "Nothing will help me. I was just born to be an anxious person."

Stress is incurable. It isn't like grief or loss that passes or fades in time. It's a normal, regularly occurring, and inevitable part of life, but it doesn't have to be avoided in order for us to be happy and healthy. If we accept that it's there and stop fighting against it so much, it affects us less. The stress will be the same, but how we react to it changes.

If you're a naturally anxious, highly sensitive, or high-energy person like me, it's also true that you'll probably deal with anxiety off and on for the rest of your life. But there's no reason to feel discouraged by that news! After all, the practice of overcoming small obstacles and stressors is what prepares us for life's biggest challenges. And as I've said, based on my own experience, we can learn to manage everyday anxiety and worry without making demands on ourselves that add to our stress levels.

I offer this to you as a person who has suffered with extreme anxiety and who has emerged out the other side—happy and at peace. Yes, happy and at peace, even though I still have some anxiety and still deal with regular stress. I'm here as proof that it can be done, and my meditation practice is how I do it!

From High Anxiety to High on Life

Just how much anxiety and stress have I learned to manage over the course of my life? When I was a kid, every night—as soon as my younger sister and I went to bed—my parents would start fighting. That was their routine. They called each other names and shouted cruel things, and it made bedtime an incredibly stressful time. I didn't even want to go to bed because I knew that was when it would start.

As a result, nightmares were another nighttime routine that persisted into my adolescence and adulthood. They became progressively more intense in theme, violence, and frequency. Nightmares allowed my stress to rise to the surface. In part because I didn't know how to process my stress and in part because I was scared, I suppressed all my so-called negative emotions and let my subconscious handle them while I slept. If I wasn't going to release those emotions willingly, my subconscious was surely going to do it for me.

I simply didn't have tools for releasing my stress, anxiety, and emotional pain in a more intentional way. I had no models for rationally expressing my emotions. I never learned the appropriate words to communicate what I was feeling. I couldn't say, "I'm sad" or "I'm angry." Screaming, name-calling, and other means of verbal violence were the only examples I was given for being heard and getting attention. In my family, if we weren't yelling, we weren't talking about our feelings at all.

When I was eight years old, I reached my limit. My parents were on their way to a divorce, but they weren't there yet. Three years before, they had decided to separate but continued living in the same house. It was agony living like that because they were still fighting constantly.

My mother was dating, which was very confusing to me, and I was forced to keep secrets from my father about it. Meanwhile, my father fell deeper into depression every day, completely withdrawing emotionally, and hardly speaking to us at all. By this time my older sister—who was like a mother to us—had moved out of the house, and my younger sister and I were basically left to fend for ourselves for everything outside of the bare minimum required for survival.

One afternoon in June—a month before my ninth birthday—I staged my first outburst. Inspired by something I had seen on TV, I pretended to see and hear "monsters." Later the doctors would call them "audio-visual hallucinations," a term that sounded very official to my eight-year-old ears—so much so that I enjoyed repeating it to all my future therapists. Those words and my list of diagnoses made me feel important. They made me feel heard.

Of course, I didn't really know what I was doing when I faked that first hallucination. I was just crying out for help, and the only way I knew how to do that was to act like I was seeing things. I started yelling and screaming, and my mother rushed me to the hospital. Her current boyfriend came along for the ride. (I think my father was at work at the time.)

I was admitted to the pediatric ward, and before I knew it, I was surrounded by a variety of psychiatrists and therapists. I was getting so much attention, and for the first time in my young life, I started to feel safe and at ease. While I don't have a lot of memories of the few days I spent in the hospital, my diary reflects a time of great excitement:

June 9, 1987
Dear Diary,
This is the first day in the Mount Holly Hospital for me. And this has already been the best day of my life. First, I got to talk on the phone. Then, I ate dinner. After that, I watched TV and played my new game. Then, my mom and her best friend got me you (diary), a bookmark, and the book The Wind in the Willows. *Well, now back to the room. It is so nice. I have my own room, my own phone, my own bathroom, and a corkboard. Well, as I would say, "life is great for me."*
Your friend,
Rebekah

Screaming, acting out violently, and staging hallucinations were the only ways that I could communicate for at least the next 10 years of my life, even after my parents divorced and I moved out of the house on my own. As counterintuitive as it seems, I didn't know any other way to get positive attention—proof that the people who were supposed to love me actually did love me. It was manic joy, a smile, or silence . . . and then periodic screaming and violent eruptions. This was my training for "managing" stress.

Not surprisingly, my first serious relationship with a boy was a violent one. Even though my parents hadn't physically abused me, it felt normal to me for my boyfriend to throw me down the stairs or slap me across the face. Oddly it was a physical release that—even when done to me—felt like the only real means of relieving the pressure inside me. My body and subconscious mind were constantly searching for new ways to deal with the stress I was feeling, but what worked in the moment never lasted long.

I saw lots of therapists, psychologists, and psychiatrists after that hospitalization when I was eight years old, and I took a number of different psychiatric medications. While I know these therapies are helpful to many people, their methods didn't help me much at all.

When I was 11 years old, however, one therapist did give me a great analogy that I still use today. He said, "It's like you're a soda bottle. Things bother you, and they shake you up. But because you have no means of release and because the cap is always on, it builds and builds until it explodes."

It was a very simple image that a child could easily understand. Still it took me years to figure out how to let the pressure out of the bottle before building to explosion. Eventually I would hear his words in my head, and I would picture my tears as the fizz you get if you turn the cap just slightly to release a tiny bit of the pressure. I had always been hesitant, if not downright scared, to cry. Crying always came with negative consequences: a frustrated reaction from my mother, another trip to the therapist, or a new prescription that would numb me even more. This soda-bottle visualization practice allowed me to release my tears in safety. It became integral to my healing and remains a constant in my stress-management routine.

Meditation as Quiet Observation

A lot of the same triggers that led me to stress and anxiety are still present in my life, but I recognize them now and choose to react differently. One of the meditations I use today includes my visualization practice of letting a little bit of pressure out of the soda bottle. It's something I can do wherever I am. I can close my eyes and twist the cap to allow some release. While it may not be a full release of all my emotions in the moment—especially if I'm in the middle of a group of people—I can manage until I have time to go into deeper meditation or delve into how I feel.

This is just one of the ways in which meditation has saved me. In my case, therapy and psychiatric drugs couldn't do it. But I don't approach meditation as a method of clearing my mind of all my negative thoughts. I don't try to use meditation to get rid of my anxiety in a given moment. Instead of quieting or emptying the mind, I approach meditation as a practice of quiet observation.

Like I said in the opening of Chapter 2, meditation is a way of saying to myself, "Yes, I see you. I recognize that you're a thinking, feeling person, and I'm here to listen." I recognize that there is an observer in me who can sit from an objective place, outside of emotion, and watch me swirl in chaotic feelings. I allow that observer in me to talk with the part of me who is caught in the middle of the stress, and in doing so, I become a friend to myself. That's all the meditation becomes for me—especially in those moments when stress or anxiety have me by the throat. And that's plenty to expect from my meditation. It's an enormous gift!

I might say to myself, "I acknowledge that you feel crazy right now. I acknowledge that things are overwhelming and that you feel a bit hopeless and stuck." But that's the end of the conversation.

I don't say, "Everything's going to be OK. Just breathe. You'll feel better." Why? Because that isn't necessarily the truth, and I don't want to put that demand on myself. Again, I don't want to layer more stress on top of the stress I'm already feeling. I want to "just be" with whatever I'm feeling and what's happening for me in that moment.

Resist the urge to go into "fix-it" mode. Do you have someone in your life who immediately tries to fix things when you have a problem? For me, that's my husband. It's a natural tendency. If someone we care about is hurting, we want to fix it. I know my husband does this for me because he loves me, so I would never blame or resent him for wanting to help. But often I don't want or need him to fix anything. I just want him to hear me and see me. I just want him to listen and acknowledge that I'm going through something difficult. Sometimes that's all I need from myself, too!

When I meditate from a place of quiet observation, it's an opportunity for me to hear and see myself right where I am in the moment. I just listen to myself and acknowledge what I'm feeling. It's a practice of unconditional, nonjudgmental compassion. I'm not trying to change anything.

Spread the Love

Meditation is a way of acknowledging that I'm a thinking, feeling person who deserves to be heard. It's a practice of self-love. #YH4M

It's natural to want to fix whatever's going "wrong." The first thing you feel the urge to do when you are anxious and out of control is to get back in control. But when you're in the middle of a storm, it's very hard to grasp on to anything. Picture yourself swirling inside a tornado. Now imagine trying to reach out and grab something to hold you steady. You'll see that it's virtually impossible.

I have found that the stress release happens for me when I allow myself to be swept up inside the tornado and simply observe myself within it. What if being in control isn't so much about holding steady or grasping on to something, but about allowing the emotions to move through me? Trying to grab hold of control and finding that I can't is what invites panic. Again, it's anxiety on top of anxiety. The layering process only makes matters worse.

Some of us try to control, and some of us try to create distance by pushing our feelings away. When we try to escape our feelings, we create a lot of tension because what we're really doing in those moments is pushing our feelings deeper inside, where they can eat away at us and maybe manifest in the subconscious or in nightmares like mine used to do. So rather than push my feelings away, I say, "I'm going to sit with these thoughts and allow my brain to just go wild." I let myself "feel all the feels"—every emotion that's there. By doing so, I release the emotions, and that eases the soda bottle's pressure so that I don't explode later.

Stillness Is Your Anchor

As your mind goes wild at first with all your feelings, fears, frustrations, and anxieties, the key is the physical stillness of meditation. You will sit still on your meditation pillow at the same time the storm is going on inside you.

One of the analogies I use is an anchor. I say, "I'm like a boat on the ocean. My faith is my anchor that holds me steady. My thoughts are like waves. I allow them to roll under me, sometimes rocking me just a bit, but I won't be carried away. I'm anchored faithfully in the here and now." You aren't stopping the waves—the anxiety, the people who let you down, or the environmental stressors that are beyond your control. You allow it all, but you aren't going to be swept away with those waves either. And again, the way to stay anchored is simply to be physically still on your pillow.

In other words, meet yourself where you are instead of trying to take yourself to another place. Perhaps you've heard that you should live in the moment, but if you're in the middle of a panic attack or terribly stressful episode, the moment doesn't feel peaceful or safe. While it can be powerful to say to yourself, "I'm safe. I'm at peace. I choose to be here," when you're in the middle of extreme chaos, the last thing you want to do is *order* yourself to feel safe. You can't *mandate* that you feel peaceful and you shouldn't judge yourself if you can't let go of the anxiety.

Living with my anxiety rather than trying to rid myself of it has given me a lot of freedom. I don't try to escape the label of "someone with anxiety." Instead I practice forgiveness and compassion toward my personality. I've been given this personality for a reason, and I don't have to reach perfection or enlightenment to be OK or lovable.

We so often receive the message that we have to shed our personalities and become perfect beings, always walking in white light. Perhaps underneath it all, we are these light beings, but it can be daunting to aspire to that level all the time. I don't know about you, but I don't feel like a being of light every day.

I'm a very sensitive person, and I absorb a lot of the emotions of the people around me. I like this aspect of my personality, and I consider my quirks and idiosyncrasies to be gifts. If I say, "I have to cure myself of my anxiety," it means I believe I'm broken. When I say, "I have anxiety," it just means that I accept that anxiety is a part of my personality at this time in my life. "Having anxiety" doesn't mean I'm broken. It doesn't define who I am as a person.

Calm in the Middle of the Storm

Before I practiced meditation, traditional therapy was how I dealt with stress. But that always kept me focused on what was outside of me. I talked about what was wrong with my life—my parents, my teachers, my siblings, my husband, and all the stressors in my environment. I was good at identifying problems outside of my control. What I hardly knew anything about was what was going on *inside* of me and how I would ever manage it well enough to be happy. What I needed was a way to work with the stress in my life rather than try to escape it or control it. I also needed to learn how to identify and manage my reactions to that stress.

I needed someone to say, "Even though you're in this abusive relationship right now, you don't have to be in another place to find some peace." I believed I couldn't start the healing process until I could get out of the relationship, but I didn't have the inner resources to get out right away. Therefore, I was stuck . . . until I learned that peace could be experienced even in the midst of chaos.

If you tell yourself that you can't experience peace because chaos is all around you, then you'll likely never experience peace. Don't put off peace until some "other time" when your world is calm and stress-free. Realistically, when is that time ever going to come? Do you know anyone who has a perfectly calm life without any stress? They might have *moments* of calm, but perfect external peace is not sustainable and not something that should be tethered to happiness.

You *can*, however, experience *internal* peace and calm on a constant basis by changing the way you relate to the stress and anxiety in your life—whether it's generated inside you or outside of you. Catch yourself if you're saying things like "I'll feel peaceful when I retire" or "I'll be stress-free when my relationship gets easier."

Spread the Love

It is my option, in every moment, to choose peace over panic. Peace is available to me, even in the midst of chaos. #YH4M

After all, we can feel stress about the best things in our lives, too, right? Getting married, having a baby, finishing a degree, and buying a new home are wonderful, exciting events, but also stressful experiences. I love my life, but with the number of children I have and everything going on each day, there's some level of chaos all the time.

What if your own situation is horrible? You can still learn to manage the stress and anxiety you experience. It has been so powerful for me to accept that I don't have to walk away from a difficult situation in order to experience calm. This doesn't mean that you should stay in a bad situation if you can leave, especially if the situation is—or has the potential to become—dangerous. If this is the case, seek help immediately. But meditation can help you focus on what's happening inside of you rather than all the awful things around you. In my own life, this practice helped me to gain clarity and muster up the inner courage to leave situations that weren't serving me.

DEALING WITH PANIC ATTACKS

How can you feel peaceful if you can't even catch your breath? I'm neither a doctor nor a psychiatrist, so this is not medical advice. As someone who has suffered from panic attacks, all I can do is simply tell you what worked for me.

Meditation posture was important for me in those moments of panic. So try sitting up tall with your chest in an open position. Don't let your body curl up in a ball. Keep your shoulders down away from your ears, and open your hands like a starfish. Part your lips, place the tip of your tongue behind your top front teeth, and let your jaw hang loose. This will help to release the muscles that you tend to clench in those situations.

Breathe and notice your breaths. This is not the time to try controlling your breaths. If they're fast and shallow, let them be. Remember that Universal law I mentioned before: once we observe something, it starts to change on its own. Continue observing your breathing by simply repeating out loud or in your head, "Inhale," on the inhales and "Exhale," on the exhales—no matter how fast they may be.

If you are able to control your breath, practicing Even Breath or One-Two Breath could be very helpful in preventing a more intense attack.

Once you have your breathing down, you can try some inner dialogue.

Instead of saying something like "I'm safe. I'm at peace. I choose to be here," focus your attention on the worst-case scenario. "Could I die?" Probably not. "I could pass out. I could start to cry. I could embarrass myself." Allow your mind to go right to the worst imaginable thing, and then accept it in the moment.

I say to myself, "That could happen, and I'm willing to go there."

If you're like me, you'll then start to recognize, "I'm not at that point yet. I'm still safe." This helps you to think more rationally. It's real and literal, in contrast to the abstract fear that has drawn you into the panic. You articulate the fear and bring it out into the open.

Our bodies react to the fear even though we aren't intellectually aware of what the fear is. Bringing it into the open often dissipates it.

During my last panic attack, I was standing in my kitchen. "I have all these bills. I have to get back to this person . . ." I had a whole list of things that were bothering me, and I almost passed out from the fear. I went to the worst-case scenario: "I could have a full nervous breakdown, and everybody around me could be let down. I could lose all my jobs and all my money and my book deal." Then I realized that the odds of any of that happening were slim, so I was able to release the fear. The pressure immediately released, and my breathing eased.

Again, it wasn't about trying to escape the panic. I named the fear and I acknowledged it. I said to myself, "I see you, Fear. I accept that you're here." Observation immediately led to change.

Allow and Reframe

Negativity gets a bad rap. Now, don't get me wrong. It deserves that bad rap most of the time, especially if we're holding on to negativity for too long. But judging ourselves for the negative words we use only creates more stress. Many of us fear that if we voice our negative feelings, we'll give them more power. We might even manifest more of the negative stuff in our lives! We can certainly manifest negativity if we dwell on it. But when we just stuff the negative feelings down into the subconscious, we actually give them more power than if we express them. We essentially become their prisoner.

So one of the best ways to keep the negativity from perpetuating itself is to let it out—clear it from our systems. When you're struggling with negativity, express it to a friend, in your journal, or silently in meditation. Then work with the positive mantras to avoid getting stuck in the negative.

Here's what I say to myself: "I'm going to really freak out for a minute, and I'm going to relieve the pressure. Then I'm going to start with a new strategy. How can I come at this with a positive perspective?"

You may be feeling overwhelmed. You may be in the middle of chaos. But that doesn't have to dictate what you do next. You can choose the words that you use, you can choose your next action, and you can choose how much you want to let your environment affect you.

The late Dr. Wayne W. Dyer—an important influence and teacher in my life—said that words like "difficult," "stressful," and "overwhelming" are only opinions. They're just descriptive words for sensations we're feeling. We can use different words to describe those sensations. How about "easy," "peaceful," and "manageable"? OK, some of those words might feel ridiculous to use, especially when you're in the middle of what feels like an impossible situation, but I'd like you to at least try to accept that there are many different ways to look at anything. And again, I'm not advocating pretending away your feelings! I want you to feel all the feels, observe them intentionally, and *only then* explore your reaction. Don't censor yourself—ever! Positivity for the sake of positivity is just denial; it doesn't erase the problem.

That said, you *could* begin to genuinely see the light in the dark. For example, it might be *difficult* for me to deal with a particularly tightly wound girlfriend in my life, but it's *easy* for me to approach her when I compliment her first or when we start by talking about something we agree on. I was able to keep my cool on my wedding day, even as things went wrong, simply by changing the words I used about it. Those words allowed me to *rename* what was happening and *reframe* my perspective on it all. I said to myself, "My husband forgot the video camera, so I'm going to be extra careful to soak up all the joy in this moment. My memories and this blissful feeling are mine no matter what, even if I don't have a permanent record of it." Once we recognize that a circumstance is outside of our control, we have an opportunity to make a choice about our reaction.

Spread the Love

When a situation is out of my control, I can struggle and complain, or I can allow and reframe. #YH4M

You'll also feel less overwhelmed if you manage your stress by taking one step at a time. "I can't get everything done, but I can cross this one thing off my to-do list." "I can't change my husband, but I can accept my feelings and worries about him by sitting still in meditation for four minutes."

The way you deal with stress will then affect the people around you and may just change your environment. I find that when I'm freaking out, my kids are also stressed out. When I meditate and manage my stress by accepting my feelings and sitting still for 4 minutes, they calm down as well.

Remember that nothing outside of you can take away your mental health. Only *your reaction* to those outside people or situations can do that. Your mental health is your own, and no one else has the right to access it. You will feel more powerful and in control when you realize that.

Are you ready to meditate? (If necessary, review the basics in Chapter 2.)

Meditation for Connecting with Ease

Preparation / About This Meditation

At no point in this book am I going to try to convince you that your stress isn't real. Your feelings have a purpose, and it would be counterintuitive to the growth process to dismiss them as unimportant. I'm also not going to tell you that your current situation is ideal. I know a lot of spiritual teachers say that, and I've been guilty of saying it, too.

Just because wherever you are is the perfect place to start doesn't mean that it's the most awesome place ever. I believe your current situation will always present as many opportunities for growth as for distraction, so it's OK to go back and forth between feeling positive and feeling like your life sucks. A card given to me by a good friend says, "We've all been to Suckville." I'm no stranger to that place. The card is permanently pinned to my inspiration board.

Your situation may look like a mess. That's real. But *you are not* that mess. That's real, too. Do you see the difference? Your surroundings are always separate from you, no matter how much of a participant you are in what's happening. Whatever responsibility you hold in how much your life is working or *seemingly* not working, who you *are* is still completely disconnected from what's happening. The essence of you never changes.

Spread the Love

We are whole beings, even when everything around us seems broken. #YH4M

I also want to say right now—before we move into the first meditation of this book—that there are going to be a lot of times when I drop some serious statements that won't feel true to you. You're going to be skeptical, and that's OK. All I ask is that you accept my statements as something that *could* be true, even if that's a *this-could-only-happen-in-a-fantasy-world* could. Make room in your heart and mind for the possibility of truth in what I'm saying, and this book will work for you.

Again, I'm never going to tell you that your feelings and opinions aren't real. I understand that what you feel is true for you in the moment, and I honor that. What I'm here to tell you is that your feelings can change. Your feelings and opinions are merely energetic things—separate from you. They are not the essence of who you are because, again, who you are doesn't change.

Every meditation in this book will start with a set of instructions. While a lot of them will sound very similar to each other, there will be specific cues assigned to each meditation for **when** and **where** to practice and which **position** to use. Don't worry about how to sit or where to look as you move on to new meditations.

When? Practice this meditation at any time of the day. If you're struggling with an ongoing stressful situation, however, you may want to create an extra layer of protection for yourself by starting your day with your meditation practice.

One of the most powerful ideas for you to grasp is that you're separate from your feelings. It's a concept that takes repeated practice to absorb. Beginning your day by planting this idea into your psyche will allow you to sort through what *is* and what *is not* you with a little more clarity. Recognizing what *is not* you allows for perspective and distance, which, in turn, creates ease.

Where? Find a quiet, comfortable spot for this meditation—at least as quiet as you can manage. Make sure that your environment supports the important work you're about to do. Accepting new concepts—especially those that may not align with your old, long-held opinions—sometimes requires a little extra help. A very noisy, chaotic space is never the place to try to get these concepts to take root. Seeds take root and grow into beautiful living things much better in a nurturing environment. And you're about to grow something beautiful! Of course, as I've said, total quiet may not be possible and isn't necessary.

Position? After you've found a quiet place to set your pillow, I want you to find your comfortable seat. This seated position is also called Easy Seat or Sukhasana. Instructions for every meditation posture, hand mudra, and the correct use of props can be found in Chapter 2. You can review those instructions all at once or just refer back to the specific pose or mudra before each meditation.

Easy Seat should feel comfortable, but it also requires you to sit up nice and tall, so energy can flow freely through your body. As soon as you're seated, you're ready for your meditation.

If you feel comfortable closing your eyes during meditation, I'd like you to close them for this one. You might be wondering how you'll be able to follow my meditations and read at the same time. I've got you covered! You can read through each meditation completely and then practice it on your own, or you can pause when directed during the meditation and refer to the next set of instructions. It will be seamless—I promise.

You Have 4 Minutes to Accept Where You Are in the Moment

Wherever you are is the perfect place to start! This place, these surroundings, this moment—all are perfect conditions for charting a new course and taking your first steps. So let's get started with your first meditation!

1. Begin by placing your attention on your breath as it is in this moment. There's no need to change your breathing to make it deeper, slower, or longer. The practice of observing your breath as it is in the present moment strengthens your meditation practice.

2. Observe how each breath feels as it passes through your nostrils, down the back of your throat, and into your lungs. Now follow it as it travels out of your body again. Spend about a minute just focusing on your breath. Your inhales and exhales flow naturally and easily. Guess what? You're already meditating. If your meditation time is spent only observing your breath, you've accomplished a lot!

3. I'm going to give you three mantras for this meditation. You'll repeat each mantra—either silently or aloud—for five full breath cycles. That's five inhales and exhales. After every inhale, repeat the mantra on your exhale. Close your eyes during the five breath cycles, and open them again briefly before proceeding to your next mantra. After your third mantra, open your eyes to read your final instruction.

Mantra 1

I am not broken or in need of fixing.

Mantra 2

I am worthy of being heard and
of being loved as I am in this moment.

Mantra 3

My inner voice is wise, and I allow
myself to listen to it without judgment.

4. Close your eyes and continue your easy inhales and exhales for as long as it feels good. Let the mantras swirl and settle as you breathe in and out, in and out. When you're ready, open your eyes and rejoin the outside world.

Meditation for Releasing Control

Preparation / About This Meditation

Ah, sweet release! I have a list of my most favorite words—scrumptious, plump, cubby, and adventure (which I use as a verb). I love these words for how they sound when I say them out loud, but also for how they make me feel inside. Of all my favorite words, though, "release" has to win the prize for the best all-around. Just saying it aloud causes every inch of my body to relax a bit. When I teach yoga, I use the cue to "release" repeatedly at the end of class to let the students know what I really want them to do with their muscles after their hard work is done.

In the same way that I guide my yoga students to create new space in their bodies by releasing physical tension, I want to offer you the idea of creating space for peace and calm by letting go of *emotional* tension, or for the purposes of this visualization meditation—pressure.

Earlier in this chapter, I told you about a tool I've used for more than two decades to help me manage my own stress and anxiety. Visualizing myself as a soda bottle has kept me from reaching a state of panic countless times over the years. If you've never tried a visualization meditation, rest assured that it's as easy as picturing something in your mind and making up a story about it. In this case, you don't even have to do it on your own. I'm going to guide you through it.

When? This is one of my in-the-moment meditations. Use it when you think you might lose it. I put this meditation in the same self-care category as "stop, drop, and roll." If I'm on fire, I'm not going to take time to ponder my place in the Universe; I'm hitting the floor and putting out the fire! My soda bottle meditation is my number one tool for situations when I feel like my own top is about to pop. It's fast, it's simple, and it works!

Where? I want you to feel like you can access this tool whenever you feel overwhelmed. I don't place a lot of importance on where you choose to practice this meditation. Use it *where* you think you might lose it. Quiet spaces are ideal for practicing meditation, but that may be an unrealistic ideal in the moment you need this meditation most.

Position? You can probably guess what I'm going to say next. Standing, sitting, lying down, pulled over on the side of the road—it's of little matter how you're positioned for this meditation. I recommend only that you be in a position that's comfortable and safe, and that you're not creating more physical tension in your body by clenching your hands or teeth. And I don't care how angry you are with the guy who just cut you off on the highway—pull over before you start meditating!

Practice with your eyes open or closed.

You Have 4 Minutes to Let It Go

Even if you don't feel like you're in danger of exploding right now, try going through each step as a trial run in preparation for a future time when you really need it. There are only two simple mantras to remember, so you'll probably be able to practice this meditation on your own after just one run-through.

1. Take a moment to draw your attention to your breath. Follow its path as it enters and exits your body—in through your nose and out through your mouth. Breathe however it feels good to you; there's no need to try to control *anything* in this moment. Everything is as it should be, even if you're feeling overwhelmed. This pressure inside of you has a purpose. It's telling you that it's time to release.

2. You're ready for your first mantra! Repeat it either silently or aloud. Match this one-word mantra to your breath. Inhale nice and easy. Then exhale and say, "Release."

3. With each exhale, notice how just a bit more tension is released from your body. Notice how your shoulders drop and how the exhale leaves your body like you're letting go of something heavy that you've been carrying for a long time. Repeat for ten full breath cycles or until your breathing has slowed to a comfortable pace.

Let's Practice Some Visualization . . .

It's so easy to release the pressure you're feeling. You're already starting to feel more at ease. You're focusing on your breath, and your first mantra has started to work its magic. Now let's work together to release any remaining pressure.

4. Picture a soda bottle with the cap tightly closed. Notice the tiny bubbles inside, rising to the surface, wanting to escape. Imagine that you're that soda bottle and that each of those tiny bubbles holds a little bit of the pressure you're feeling right now. If the cap stays closed, the bubbles pop inside, and the pressure is reabsorbed. Let's set that pressure free.

5. Continue to pay attention to your inhales and exhales. Now instead of repeating a mantra on your exhale, visualize the cap of your soda bottle twisting just enough that a little bit of "fizz" is released. Even more bubbles are rushing to the surface, ready to escape the bottle and disappear into the outside air. Inhale through your nose, and then exhale out through your mouth. The cap loosens further, and a bit more pressure is released. Continue this pattern until no more bubbles remain and it's safe to open the cap completely. You are now able to breathe easily, and all the pressure is gone.

Sealing Your Practice and Allowing Your Meditation to Take Root . . .

Your sealing mantra is "It isn't my job to be in control. I accept what is." If you're comfortable repeating this out loud, do it. Otherwise, repeat it silently to yourself on each exhale for three full breath cycles. These words will seal your practice and allow you to continue to release pressure whenever it bubbles up throughout your day.

Meditation for Peace and Calm

Preparation / About This Meditation

The purpose of meditation—especially for those struggling with stress and anxiety—is to learn how to focus attention on fewer and fewer things until the focus is placed on only one thing. Repeating mantras, using visualization, and practicing simple breathing techniques are just a few methods that allow you to free yourself from the distraction of a busy mind and a chaotic environment. Once you've created a regular practice and can focus your attention on a single thought, you'll find that accessing inner peace is easy.

A lot of people think meditation is about relaxation, but feeling relaxed is just another delicious bonus of the important work that's being done. Peace and calm is accessed through careful attention. Peace, as defined in the dictionary, is the freedom of the mind from annoyance, distraction, and anxiety. Learning to train your focus in the midst of unsettling events outside of your control is the essence of a meditation practice that can carry you peacefully and calmly through any challenging time.

So what does all this mean? Stress and chaos are inevitable parts of life. We all deal with some degree of them every day. Ironically, chaos is pretty predictable. We can't control when it shows up, but we can prepare ourselves for when it does. For instance, the ocean is a wild, unpredictable, and sometimes dangerous place, but we can always depend on the ebb and flow of the tides. You don't have to be a psychic to know when to pick up the beach towels and head home. Signs of a storm brewing are a cue to drop anchor and lower the sails. To ignore the signs would be deadly. If we can't find a way to anchor ourselves energetically, we'll be swept away into a dark ocean of chaotic distraction. Allow your steady seat and this meditation to be your energetic anchor in rough emotional seas.

When? Whether you find yourself in a brief moment of feeling overwhelmed, or you're trying to navigate your way through an ongoing stressful situation, this meditation can serve you well. Do it in the morning to anchor yourself in peace before you're inundated with external stress or before internal stress takes over your thoughts. The ebb and flow of stress is predictable. Storms can come on suddenly, but rarely out of nowhere. You can be ready for it all.

Where? Create a protection for yourself with this meditation in the safety of your own peaceful environment. Recognize your chosen meditation space as a sacred place where stress is acknowledged and dealt with, but never indulged. Keep it clean and uncluttered. The calmer the environment, the easier it will be for you to deal with whatever chaos is happening around or inside you.

Position? Sit up nice and tall in your Easy Seat. Remember that you always have the option of using the Chair Meditation Pose if sitting cross-legged or on the floor is uncomfortable for you. Also feel free to use any props that help support better spinal alignment and greater comfort while sitting.

Place the palms of your hands on your knees or thighs.

We're aiming to remove distractions here, so try to practice this meditation with your eyes closed or with them open and focused on a single object. I'll instruct you to refer back to the written meditation after each set of breath cycles.

You Have 4 Minutes to Find Stillness in Chaos

You're about to enter a sacred space of safety and protection. I'm going to offer you visualization cues to help you settle into place, and I'll give you a mantra to repeat at the end. This mantra will seal your practice and offer you protection from anything that tries to "rock your boat."

Let's begin with you sitting up tall in your Easy Seat.

1. Inhale and exhale three times. With each inhale, lift your shoulders up toward your ears. With each exhale, roll your shoulders back and drop your shoulder blades down along your spine.

2. Your seat is your energetic anchor; make it strong. Be sure that the crown of your head is pointed toward the sky, your chest is open, and your shoulders are broad and positioned right above your hips.

You Are a Boat on the Ocean . . .

Before closing your eyes, let me help you set your scene. After you've imagined the scene completely, there will be time to close your eyes and allow your visualization to take hold.

3. You're sitting in a small, wooden boat tied to a tiny dock on the shore of a beautiful, tropical beach. The sun is low in the sky, and the horizon is vibrant with hues of red, orange, and hot pink. The water is choppy, the breeze is steady through the trees, and the sound of seabirds fills the air. There's a lot to see, feel, and hear. It's a peaceful but active place.

4. Feel your boat rocking gently in the choppy water. The rocking comforts you because you know you're safe inside the boat. With each wave that rolls into shore, the water becomes less and less choppy. Your boat rocks gentler.

5. Imagine that any thoughts or worries that enter your mental space are being carried in and out on those waves. As the wave rolls out, it carries the thought and leaves it to the vastness of the ocean, never to be seen again.

6. Close your eyes, and for ten full breaths or until the water is completely calm, inhale and exhale as the waves roll into shore and then disappear into the ocean. Then open your eyes to read your mantra.

Your Meditation Draws to a Close . . .

Read the following mantra three times silently or out loud. Allow yourself to read it slowly, fully absorbing the meaning and energy of the words. Make sure to take a nice, long breath in between each repetition.

Your sealing mantra "I'm like a boat on the ocean. My faith is the anchor that holds me steady. My thoughts are like waves. I allow them to roll under me, sometimes rocking me just a bit, but not carrying me away. I'm anchored faithfully in the here and now."

Chapter 4

4 Minutes to Fulfill the Dream of Great Self-Esteem

The anxiety I experienced when I was younger became severe social anxiety during my tween and teen years. I couldn't even ask for extra napkins at a restaurant or order a pizza over the phone.

It may have been learned behavior to some degree. My father had had a traumatic childhood and was afraid of being in public. He seemed to be able to handle the outside world only for work and church. He avoided everything else, including my art exhibits and graduations. He'd always have some excuse, such as, "People will judge me because I don't have the right clothes to wear." He was so preoccupied with the opinions of other people that even getting him to attend my wedding was a battle, which I won only after I offered to buy him clothes for the entire weekend of events. Feeling compassion toward him was hard. His social anxiety exhausted me, but it also became ingrained in my own psyche.

The message that he wasn't good enough—and, therefore, *we* weren't good enough—was loud and clear throughout my life. I always had an acute understanding that we were the poor family in the neighborhood, the "trash on the block." Some of that could have been imagined and exaggerated, of course, but there was no question that people saw us that way to at least some degree.

Due to my parents' financial situation, their need to work so much, and the disarray of their marriage, our home was in equal disarray. The grass was always growing too high. The house and the yard always looked a mess. At one point we even had an old claw-footed bathtub on the front yard that my father never bothered to install. It remained there for years, filling with dirt and debris, rusting, and eventually becoming a makeshift fort for the neighborhood kids. It finally lost its home when a neighbor was expecting visitors and asked if we could move the bathtub from the yard to the porch. She was that embarrassed by it. But the message I received was that *we* were the real source of her embarrassment.

Even to this day, I feel a tiny pang of humiliation as I write about this. Every time I drive up my current driveway and the front of my home comes into view, my heart swells with joy. I wonder if this joy is made bigger by the fact that my home's appearance contrasts so greatly with the house of my childhood. The manicured lawn and the neat porch lined with white rocking chairs would have looked like a dream to my child self's eyes.

The counter to all the negative stuff that I just told you is that in my early childhood, my parents were churchgoers—born-again Christians—who repeated many times to us: "It doesn't matter what anyone else thinks of you. You're children of God, and God loves you just as you are." Because of that alone, I was told I was destined for great things. While the environment was neglectful to a large degree, my parents always loved me and supported me for who I was. Even though they didn't hold themselves in such high regard, I was considered a treasure. I was never ridiculed. I was never told I wasn't good enough. I was always told I was created by God, and that meant something big for my future.

Because I knew that God loved me in spite of whatever judgments others had of me, it was almost as if I had a secret power. I was able to connect with God directly through a constant prayer practice, and that made me feel special. Even when the chaos of my environment was overwhelming—which it often was—I used my secret power to ground myself for at least a moment.

But around the time that my sexuality started to develop, my secret power dissolved along with it. My secret power was no match for the vulnerability and the emotional and physical upheaval of puberty. If I had been able to stay connected to the knowledge that God loved me unconditionally, I truly believe it would have carried me into my teen years and adulthood and prevented me from a lot of turmoil.

But like most of us in our early teens, I allowed my self-worth to become attached to the opinions of others. As I started to notice that my clothes and my circumstances were different from the other kids, my peers became a bigger voice than my parents or even God. I imagined that everyone saw me as poor or worthless or ugly. This feeling of being "less than" persisted, and my circumstances nurtured its rapid growth.

Since I grew up in a very small town, I couldn't pretend about my family's situation. If I couldn't get new shoes at the beginning of a school year, I'd have to wear dirty, old shoes. Or a teacher would drop off my homework at our house and see how we lived. Or my father would have to come to school for some reason, and everyone would see that he didn't have teeth. It was mortifying, and there was no place to hide.

So I went from having this secret superpower that made me feel limitless and with a special future ahead of me . . . to very abruptly feeling like I had no future at all. Feeling completely disconnected from my source left me untethered and without purpose, like a balloon floating directionless, vulnerable to being guided solely by the whimsy of the wind. My detachment from God or Source, and my attachment to the opinions of others, effectively destroyed my self-esteem.

The degree to which I loved myself was dependent upon the impulses of my peers, whose emotions were bouncing off the walls. And my own feelings—also bouncing off the walls—affected my self-worth, too. On a dime, I'd go from being praised by a teacher to classmates laughing at me for being poor or making fun of my parents or putting me down because of my clothes. Attaching my value as a person to both the positive and negative opinions of others meant that my sense of self-worth was on a roller coaster, and the slightest thing could send me over the edge.

I wasn't prepared as a young person to deal with that, so the ridicule led to hopelessness and despair. Constantly riding an emotional roller coaster overwhelmed my senses and caused me tremendous pain. I didn't believe I would even live past my 20s. I didn't think I was worthy of the life that God had given me. I felt confused about my purpose and my place in the world. I suffered tremendous pain from the bad feelings I harbored about myself, and I felt guilt about the ingratitude I was showing toward God.

The short view of my prepubescent mind kept me from being able to see any light at the end of the tunnel. I couldn't imagine that life could change for me. The chaos at home and the bullying at school were too much for me to bear, and I became suicidal. I was only 10 years old when I first tried to kill myself. Emergency interventions followed—a 30-day stint in a group home, outpatient psychiatric treatments, and experiments with prescription drugs—but they were only distractions that kept me temporarily safe. I was still suffering on the inside, and this manifested in behaviors that put me in harm's way again and again.

I thought every single person in my life was allowed to have an opinion about who I was and about my value as a person. By being so open and so hungry for love, I allowed everybody in. It was a slippery slope that eventually led me to allow boys and young men to take advantage of me. I frequently placed myself in dangerous situations. I was almost date-raped after a night of underage drinking, and as I mentioned in the last chapter, I entered into a physically abusive relationship at the tender age of 15. I drank and used drugs excessively without regard for my physical safety, and eventually I married a man who was as damaged as I was. I remained in a manic, mutually abusive, and ultimately self-destructive relationship with him for a decade.

I didn't drink, do drugs, or enter into sexual relationships because I wanted to, but because I thought it was expected of me. I thought it would bring me the love and acceptance I so desperately needed.

When I allowed my self-worth to be all about what others thought of me, I lost control and allowed others to treat me in whatever way they wanted. Now I know that it's our job to teach people how to treat us and how to love us, but in my younger years, I didn't realize that responsibility. I unintentionally gave away my power.

When tweens and teens give in to this kind of peer pressure, it's because of self-esteem. It isn't because they weren't raised with proper morals and values. It isn't because they're unloved or hopelessly damaged. It could simply be that they've attached their self-worth to the opinions of other people, and the reward of acceptance is worth any emotional or even physical risk.

Without a strong sense of self and personal value, any young person can be led to behave in a self-destructive manner. And all too often, even into adulthood, we don't learn to center our self-esteem within ourselves. We still think it's all about how other people see us.

But true self-esteem has to be generated within. If we base our self-worth on others' opinions, we'll always be starved. We'll always be looking for someone else to validate us and feed that ravenous beast inside who doesn't believe we're worthy. Then, on the days when we can't find someone to tell us how great we are, we feel lost.

Even when someone tells us we're great, we don't really believe it if we don't have a strong anchor of inner self-esteem. Compliments seem to need something to attach to within us before they'll take hold. Otherwise we discard the kind words as untrue. Only when a compliment from someone else reaffirms what we already believe about ourselves does it have an impact that can help us feel stronger in our self-loving.

Spread the Love

Compliments serve me only when they're affirmations of a true inner knowing. My love for myself is a magnet for love from others. #YH4M

You Are Loved "As Is"

I'm lucky I survived the dangerous things I did when I was younger. For a long time, I felt ashamed of my behavior during those years. It was hard to see myself in the present because I constantly judged myself for the past. Today I'm a woman who's happily married with five beautiful children and a great career. But even today, the memory of who I was can block me from fully accepting and loving myself . . . *if I let it.*

Many of us move on and create lives for ourselves that look nothing like who we were before, but we keep a foot or maybe even just a toe in that old life, making us feel as though we're still not good enough. We carry old shame from a time when we made decisions not based on self-love or love for others.

Is there any part of your past that you feel shame about? It could be from 20 years ago. It could be from last week. Speaking now from a place of love, what would you say to the part of you who made those mistakes in the past?

There's no one in my life who's perfect in every way, yet I love many people deeply and completely. Just like those we love in all their glorious imperfections, we can learn to love and forgive our past selves, knowing that we did the best we could at the time.

In the last chapter, I said negativity often gets a bad rap, and I meant it! But it's also true that if we want to treat ourselves better and teach others how to treat us, we need to take it easy on the negative self-speak. As I said before, we need to give the negative feelings voice . . . and then quickly turn them around.

In our society, we don't think twice about saying negative things about ourselves. In fact, people are praised for self-deprecating humor and admonished as boastful or conceited if they speak with pride about their own achievements. How often do you speak poorly about yourself in front of others? No matter how innocent the intention, this is a dangerous practice. It's contagious, and if left unchecked, it can spread to everyone around you. Even if you're joking, you inadvertently invite other people to think of you that way and to treat you that way, too. In fact, you're hypnotizing them to *believe* your negative self-speak, even if they didn't before.

Just like we use positive mantras over and over again to create new beliefs in ourselves, repeatedly using negative words about ourselves in front of other people creates new beliefs in their minds. If people hear you say, "Oh, I'm so stupid," or "I'm too fat," you unconsciously give them permission to think, believe, and even say the same about you out loud. Of course, if someone actually called you fat or ugly or stupid to your face, you probably wouldn't stand for it. So why do you stand for it when you say it about yourself?

How can you tell the difference between honest self-reflection and self-abuse? Ask yourself, "How would I feel if these statements were coming from someone else? Would I accept and recognize them as compassionate criticism, or would they feel like insults?" Meditate on the answer carefully before labeling the statements as helpful or hurtful. But once you have the answer, proceed accordingly. Honor the helpful, and kick those self-hating statements to the curb.

In meditation I use mantras that help me learn to love myself as I am—unconditionally. I don't have to know everything to be lovable. I don't have to do everything right to be lovable. When I forget and say something negative about myself, I make it a practice to immediately remind myself with loving mantras that I don't have to be perfect to be lovable.

I also extend that love to all my past selves, including the young me who repeatedly got into trouble. I affirm: "I love the me who did drugs—just as she was." "I love the me who messed up that relationship—just as she was." "I love the me who said that hateful thing—just as she was." Even if I don't quite believe it at first, I say it anyway. Our negative self-speak has become such a bad habit that it makes sense to create a new, better habit—even if it means we have to fake it a little in the beginning.

In time, you can learn to love yourself as God or Source or the Universe (whichever term you prefer) loves you. Give yourself the same love that God gives you. One of my favorite mantras is "God loves me as is." This mantra can then evolve into "I love myself as is."

TAKE ACTION NOW: SCHEDULE A DATE WITH YOURSELF

What I didn't understand at a young age was that loving myself required action. Over time, through my meditation practice and through learning how to recognize my self-worth, I came to understand that loving myself is something I have to demonstrate outwardly, just as I do in my relationships with others. I regularly show my husband, children, and friends how much they mean to me. I have to do the same with myself.

When I demonstrate self-love, I not only reaffirm my own self-worth but I also show other people how to treat me. If I don't constantly show other people how much I love myself, they won't be inspired to love me in a way that feels good to me. I show them how I care for myself by taking time for meditation every single day, treating myself well with experiences I enjoy (including going out by myself when I need it), and speaking kindly about myself. And in doing so, I model for my children how to treat themselves with love.

I even take myself out on dates! The first time I took myself "on a date" to the movies, it felt so weird. But once I settled in with my favorite snacks, it felt really good. I was paying attention to me and me alone, and that attention was something I truly needed. There was a simple sweetness in that act of treating myself that I hadn't experienced before.

Now I take myself on dates all the time to the bookstore, cafés, or Target. (Yes, Target equals romance for me! I'll bet a lot of you feel the same.) I wander and wonder and spend time with myself, always keeping in mind that the point is pleasure. Just as I would be especially attentive to a romantic interest's needs, I'm attentive to my own. I say yes to myself and seek out experiences that nurture my desires.

I don't run errands or take phone calls on my solo dates. I make sure I look cute, and I make a point to smile a lot. My dates with myself are all about me taking care of me. They feel silly and self-indulgent and wonderful, and I highly recommend that you put one on your calendar right now!

Pretend that you're taking yourself out on a date. No yoga pants allowed! Dress up for yourself, and think about what interests you. What kind of date would excite you? What are your favorite places, movies, foods, and activities? Plan the perfect adventure and take it solo—just for you.

Does going out sound like a chore? If so, stay in. Self-care at home is an amazing way to treat yourself—light some candles, soak in the tub, fix your favorite meal, or binge-watch an entire series on Netflix. Design an experience for yourself like you would for the love of your life. It can create huge shifts in the way you see yourself and care for your own needs.

You Were Created with Divine Intention

Once you begin to experience moments of loving yourself unconditionally, take it a step further and affirm that your existence is important and on purpose, saying "I was created with divine intention."

Bishop T. D. Jakes says, "You were commanded to be fruitful. You could not be fruitful if you didn't have the seeds. You have greatness inside of you." If we were created with loving and divine intention, as I believe, we were also given the tools to do great things. As we clear the need to measure our worth by the opinions of others, we clear the obstacles to our greatness.

Spread the Love

I am whole. I am worthy. I am lovable.
I was created with divine intention. #YH4M

The painful experiences that I had as a result of not loving myself have been like fertilizer that helped the seeds I was given to grow into fruit. And that fruit is the expression of my greatness. Fertilizer is smelly and dirty, of course. We don't want to handle it, but it has a profound purpose. Without it, growth would be impossible.

I have a tiny worm farm in my house right now (it's as weird as it sounds), and the worms create worm castings (poop) in the soil, which is an amazing natural fertilizer for my garden. Meanwhile my neighbors enthusiastically collect manure from the local horse farms every spring and fall to ensure the seeds they sow in their gardens grow, become fruitful, and multiply. This manure, the muck of life, is the fertilizer that helps all the beauty of our gardens come to fruition. What most would see as castoff has tremendous value to those trying to create something new, beautiful, and nourishing.

So as I look back on my past and affirm my love for my former selves, I also say, "Thank you so much for the lessons you taught me. Thank you for that stinky fertilizer!" I can only be grateful because that emotional muck was the fertilizer that strengthened my resolve and grew my happiness. I will never underestimate the value of my "stinky stuff" again. I came out the other side of all it empowered and happy. You can, too.

Using Meditation to Increase Self-Love

I recently took my four-year-old to register for preschool, and the teacher told me about their art class. Half of the art instruction is rigidly structured, giving the kids specific steps to follow. That raised a concern in me. When we're taught "how" to create, we start to lose our own point of view. I immediately recalled when I was a little girl and how free it felt when there were no rules as to how I expressed myself. Who were you when there were no rules or ideas about how you "should" be?

When I have crises of confidence, I go into a meditative state and ask, "When did I feel good about myself?" I take myself back to that time when I felt strong—tapping into that feeling of freedom once again. For some of us, it may require going back to age two or three when we felt freedom of expression without hindrance. When did you still hold a core belief that you were worthy? When did your worth not fluctuate based on what your parents or friends thought of you?

Ask yourself: Who would I be if I weren't scared of other people's opinions? What would my day look like? How would I talk? How would I carry myself? What opportunities would I pursue?

Today I understand that what others think of me really isn't my business. *My* business is my personal growth and strengthening my own love for myself. I can accept compassionate criticism and consider it with an intellect that works in partnership with a loving heart. I can be aware of what others think of me, but I don't have to let their opinions affect me. And I can still be a sensitive person who can tap into the vibes of other people, but those vibes don't change my sense of value or self-worth. Vibes fluctuate, but my value is steady. This is not a one-time lesson. It's a constant practice to maintain that steady sense of value, and meditation is what brings me back to my own core of self-love over and over again.

Every day I challenge myself to love who I am no matter what. Something unpleasant happened—can I love myself anyway? And can I love myself now? . . . How about now?

I feel that it's my responsibility to love myself. I was created to be something great, and it's my job to keep navigating around the obstacles to access that greatness. It's an awe-inspiring responsibility, not one that causes pressure or overwhelms me. It's exciting, and it's the most nourishing gift we can give ourselves.

Meditation for Manifesting Support

Preparation / About This Meditation

Your meditation practice is a beautiful expression of self-love. It also has the potential to teach all the people who love you. When I hide out in my laundry room and tell the kids it's "mommy time," I'm communicating something very important: *I deserve time just for me. I'm special and worthy of attention. Self-care is a priority in my life.*

I'm speaking from my experience as a mom, but I'm sure you can relate to feeling a little guilty about taking time for yourself. With so much to do every single day, carving out time just to feel good may seem selfish or self-indulgent. But here's the truth: self-care is nonnegotiable for happy people. And the people who love you will learn to respect your practice. When children see it on a regular basis, they grow up learning to respect themselves and their own self-care.

How we speak about ourselves is also an aspect of self-care. This meditation will help you create more loving conversations about yourself in your mind, which will manifest as words you use in conversations. Your friends, family, and everyone you encounter will be inspired by your free and easy expressions of self-love. You will teach others how to love you better and how to love themselves better.

When? Morning is a wonderful time to imprint loving intentions into your subconscious. Hopefully nothing has gotten in the way yet of a perfectly good day, and distractions are at a minimum. If you live with other people, you may have to get up just five to ten minutes earlier to make sure your meditation time goes undisturbed. Waking up before everyone else and securing a quiet space for your practice is a great habit to adopt.

Where? If your bedroom is a quiet space, meditate there. Try to fit this meditation into your morning schedule before you do anything else. If you can do it as soon as you wake up—perfect! If you share your bedroom, any other quiet space will work just fine.

Position? Grab your pillow and position yourself in Easy Seat. Sitting up tall in this posture will encourage the positive flow of energy throughout your body.

This is the first time that I'm suggesting using a hand mudra, so take a moment to refer back to Chapter 2 for instructions on how to create the Cup/Chalice Mudra with your hands and fingers. This mudra will help you create a sense of balance, connection to self, and steadiness in your seat.

You Have 4 Minutes to Attract Loving Support

Let's start the day with love. During this meditation I'll ask you to focus your attention on your heart center (the middle of your chest). You'll also do some work with visualization and your Heart Chakra.

1. Sitting tall in your seat, take five deep, cleansing breaths—in through your nose and out through your mouth. Inhales will cause your chest to rise and your belly to expand. Exhales exit your body quickly, releasing any tension inside. Continue with your natural breath, which is now more relaxed and even.

    Follow this and the remaining steps with your eyes closed, or open and focused on a single object. Read each step completely before closing or focusing your eyes, and then refer to the text again after each step to receive your next instruction.

Shine Your Own Bright Light . . .

2. Imagine yourself surrounded by glowing ribbons of white light. As you inhale and exhale peacefully, the

light swirls gently around you and comes together as an orb, hovering above your head. Follow the light as it enters your body through the crown of your head and settles in your heart center. Focus your attention on the light in your heart as it changes into a glowing, green orb. Spend a few breath cycles just watching the green light expand and contract with your inhales and exhales.

3. Continue to focus your attention on your glowing green orb as you repeat the following three mantras. Each mantra should be repeated on the exhale for five full breath cycles. After each set of five breaths, open your eyes, read the next mantra, and then continue for another set of breaths.

Mantra 1

I love taking care of myself.

Mantra 2

Pleasure is my priority.

Mantra 3

Loving myself teaches others how to love me.

4. Keep your eyes closed and your attention focused on your heart center. Continue to breathe naturally. Notice how your breathing is deeper, calmer, and more peaceful than when you first began. Notice how your green orb is glowing brighter. Your loving intention has given your light even more energy. Allow yourself to stay this way for as long as it feels good. When you're ready, open your eyes and begin your day.

Meditation for Empowerment

Preparation / About This Meditation

"Strong fences make good neighbors." This proverb applies to literal fences and to the boundaries we create around our hearts, too. Fences are not brick walls. We can peek over them and reach beyond them. It's smart to have a gate to sometimes walk through or to allow a friend to visit our side. Fences don't necessarily have to hide us or shut us off from the world. They simply mark a boundary—real or imaginary.

When our boundaries are clear, it's easier to communicate and take action in ways that serve both sides—little is left for debate. Healthy relationships flourish when boundaries are honored. Likewise, when you create agreements with yourself about what you *are* and *are not* willing to tolerate, you're less likely to place yourself in negative or stressful situations. You take care of yourself by honoring your own boundaries.

Sometimes it's hard work maintaining the boundaries you've created. People may try to push past them, or you may feel guilty about defending them. It's natural to want to be liked, and it never feels good to offend someone. But boundaries serve an important purpose. They keep you from wandering off course—or worse, straight off a cliff! Meditation is a perfect time to contemplate the agreements you've made with yourself and reinforce that it's OK to set energetic boundaries between other people and you.

When? I don't know about your situation, but the people in my life who don't value me and who challenge my boundaries don't do it on a schedule. I wish they did. Then I could hide behind a brick wall and not a fence—maybe shut off the lights and pretend I'm out.

So practice this meditation as needed. Maybe you're dealing with a difficult person or situation that you can't avoid, and this meditation will become part of your regular practice. Maybe you're just fired up over a particular incident when you gave away your power and were left feeling angry or diminished. This meditation will also work in moments of acute frustration.

Where? Practice in as quiet a space as you can, free from any (agitating) distractions. Birds tweeting and gentle breezes? Good. Kids yelling and phones ringing? Not so good. But if you need it while at work or elsewhere, go right ahead.

Position? Wherever you are, choose a seat that feels strong. If you're seated on the floor or a pillow in Easy Seat, sit up nice and tall with your chest open wide, the crown of your head pointed toward the sky, and your shoulders positioned over your hips. You may also use the Chair Meditation Pose if you're at work. Workplaces tend to be hotbeds for power struggles and boundary pushes. Feel free to tack a copy of this meditation on your office bulletin board as a public service announcement (complete with a winking-face emoji, of course).

Place the palms of your hands on your knees or thighs.

I recommend practicing this meditation with your eyes closed.

You Have 4 Minutes to Establish Healthy Boundaries

You're about to rock this meditation with some serious power. Strong boundaries allow your heart to sing freely. You're safe and you're free to express yourself however you'd like. You're free to feel good and be loved as you are.

1. Focus on your breath as it is right now. Is it calm and even? Quick and labored? Spend a few moments just observing your breath and its alignment with how you're feeling emotionally and physically in this moment.

2. Now create an even stronger seat. Lift the crown of your head higher toward the sky, broaden your shoulders, open your chest, and feel your bottom rooted down toward the earth.

3. Begin practicing Even Breath—match the length of your inhales and exhales. Practice Even Breath with your eyes closed (if you can) for seven full breath cycles, measuring the length of your inhales and exhales. If it feels good, you can measure by counting.

4. Repeating your mantras out loud will send a powerful message to the Universe that you're serious. Repeat each mantra on the exhale for five full breath cycles. After each set of breath cycles, open your eyes and read your next mantra.

Mantra 1

I say no to things that don't serve me.
I say yes when something feels good.

Mantra 2

I create healthy boundaries for myself.

Mantra 3

I invest in relationships with people
who love and respect me as I am.

5. Notice how good it felt to say those statements out loud. Or if you said them silently, notice how they've been absorbed by every cell in your body. You're sitting up tall, and your posture is powerful and energized. You're radiating positive vibrations.

6. Finally, close your eyes for three giant, letting-go breaths. Inhale through your mouth, and then release every bit of breath from your body with a big exhale. When you're finished, open your eyes. The day is yours!

Meditation for Ultimate Self-Love
and Calling in Purpose

Preparation / About This Meditation

You were created with divine intention. That is an indisputable, undeniable fact. You are a miraculous being capable of great things, and your life has a unique purpose. Discovering that purpose is one of your most important jobs in this lifetime.

This meditation for ultimate self-love isn't about identifying that purpose, though. Its function is to help you wholeheartedly believe that your purpose exists and that you're deserving of finding it. That's it! Once you believe that you have a purpose, you create opportunities for your purpose to reveal itself to you. So think of this meditation as a welcome sign for your purpose. You're sending a signal into the ether that says, "Hey, Purpose! I know you're out there (or already in here), and I want to be friends! You're welcome to show up at any time!"

Purpose isn't a fan of showing up for people who are unsure of themselves, so this meditation will also help you cultivate some hot, steamy, radical self-love to attract your purpose. This will happen over a three-step process. I'll guide you through three mantras—one for detaching yourself from opinions, one for making declarations of your worthiness, and one for attracting the attention of your purpose.

When? Dreams do a great job of helping us work through our "stuff" and influencing us on a subconscious level. Why not meditate before bed and give your dreams *good* material to use? A nighttime meditation makes your last thoughts of the day good thoughts. Instead of just dreaming about "whatever," you can reprogram your subconscious for self-love. Finish all the other parts of your nighttime routine before settling in for this meditation. It should be the last thing you do before falling asleep.

Where? Try it in bed! You're going to seal this meditation with sleep, so your bed might be the perfect spot. Make sure your bedroom is peaceful, quiet, and dark (you may have to use a small book light to read this meditation on your first attempt).

His Holiness the 14th Dalai Lama said, "Sleep is the best meditation." Creating a space perfect for sleep is basically the same as creating one for meditation. So how do you do that? Start by removing everything that rings, beeps, or buzzes. This was so hard for me! I used to sleep with my phone under my pillow and check it several times throughout the night and first thing in the morning. There were nights when I would fall asleep with it still in my hand!

Treat yourself better than that! Leave your phone, laptop, and all other electronics outside your bedroom door. If you're someone who cannot wake up without help, get a simple alarm clock—don't use the one on your phone. You may have a partner who insists on having a TV in the bedroom. Make a compromise that screens go off at a certain time, and suggest that you both read something light before bed.

Your senses are awake even when you're asleep, so having a TV or music playing only stimulates you and interrupts deep sleep. If you think falling asleep to the TV is working for you, I assure you it isn't. Make your bedroom as dark as possible—no flickering screens, night-lights, or streetlights shining through your windows. Turn it off, tune it out, and enjoy the silence.

Position? You can lean back against some pillows in your Easy Seat or try a supported position like Semireclined Bound Angle Pose. It's OK to feel relaxed, but don't get so relaxed that you fall asleep just yet!

Allow your hands to rest on your knees or thighs with palms upturned, or to rest at your sides if you're in a reclined position.

You'll be guided to close your eyes before each mantra. After repeating the third mantra, keep your eyes closed and drift off to sleep.

You Have 4 Minutes to Invite Purpose

This is a major meditation! You're going to make huge declarations that will take root and support every one of your dreams. Discovering your purpose is monumental and the journey to that discovery can be full of adventure. The more open you are, the more you fall in love with yourself, and the easier it is for you and your purpose to find each other. So, let's call Purpose in!

1. Allow yourself to breathe naturally. Don't attempt to manipulate your breath. Just notice your breath entering and exiting your body with ease. Continue to focus on your breath until you notice that it has become peaceful and even.

2. Now that you're settled in your comfortable seat, begin to relax even further by closing your eyes and mentally scanning your entire body from your crown to your toes. Starting at the top of your head, allow your attention to travel down your body, noticing any tension or discomfort. Scan your forehead, eyes, and jaw. Release all the muscles of your face, and part your lips. As your attention passes over your shoulders, chest, and arms, let go of all tension. Allow your fingers to open and relax. Let your belly be loose—don't hold it in. Scan your thighs, and allow your attention to travel all the way down through your legs to your toes. Wiggle your toes, and let everything go.

Thoughts for Sweet Dreams . . .

It's time to repeat your ultimate self-love mantras. Each of these mantras is absolutely true. The faster you accept the undeniable truth of these mantras, the closer you are to connecting with your purpose.

Repeat each mantra on the exhale of each of five full breath cycles. After you've repeated each set of breath cycles, open your eyes to read your next mantra. At the end of your last set of breaths, say good night to the Universe. It's time to put your subconscious to work for you while you enter a deep, restful sleep. If you've been using a small light to read, shut it off before repeating your last mantra.

Mantra 1

When I detach from others' opinions,
I connect with my truth.

Mantra 2

I am divine love and infinite possibility.

Mantra 3

I'm ready to connect with my purpose.

Chapter 5

4 Minutes to
Accept Your Body

Women tell me all the time, "I'm working really hard to love my body, and it just isn't working. What's wrong with me?"

We've just talked about increasing your self-love, but loving your body is an especially difficult task these days. After all, the images of "perfect" bodies are everywhere—on the sides of buses, at the grocery store checkout line, on television, on Facebook, in website ads. They're relentless. Even though we know these photos of models and actresses have been Photoshopped, it's hard not to compare ourselves to them . . . and come up short.

Yet somehow we're supposed to counteract all these pictures of thin perfection and love our bodies no matter what. At least that's what the endless well-meaning memes that fill my Facebook page tell me: "Love your body," "Your body hears everything your mind says, so stay positive," "Every body is a bikini body." (That last one usually shows up right next to an ad for a product promising to get me bikini ready within two weeks.) Not only are we bombarded with impossible standards of beauty, but we're also told it isn't OK to dislike our bodies.

We beat ourselves up for not looking perfect . . . and then we beat ourselves up for beating ourselves up. It's that whole nasty layering thing again—anxiety on top of anxiety on top of anxiety. And the last thing women need is another source of stress!

Whether the message is negative or positive, we stay preoccupied with how we look . . . or how we feel about how we look . . . or how we feel about how other people feel about how we look. It's an epidemic that has made us hyperaware of appearances. Sometimes I just want to scream, "Enough!"

Have you ever felt like that? Can you relate?

Well, here's your ticket off that hamster wheel: *I give you permission to hate your body.* That's right—it's OK if you don't like the way you look. (Did you just exhale?) I know, I know—I just insisted that you stop negative self-speak. But this is an area where we put way too much pressure on ourselves to be positive.

Remember I said that negativity gets a bad rap. But don't get me wrong. I would never tell you that it's *good* to feel *bad* about yourself for a prolonged period of time, but I *am* telling you that the road to loving your body is not paved with denial about your true feelings. I'm reinforcing that theme because it's so important. We've been taught that feeling bad about ourselves is abnormal. But if it's abnormal, there may not be a normal person on the planet!

If you're anything like me, there are days when you just have to say, "No, I can't love my cellulite today, and you can't make me!" Some days I just want to feel like it's OK to feel bad about myself for a little while. That's the truth of the moment, and trying to pretend it doesn't exist does nothing but sweep it under the rug. (If I'm not careful, I can end up with a big pile under that rug!)

Rather than hide the negativity from myself, my strategy is to work toward *accepting and allowing it.* "Today I hate how I look." There it is. That's the reality. The liberation is in the allowing!

Start from where you are without judgment. Approach the thought with curiosity instead of disdain. Try simply observing it: "Hmmm . . . I hate how I look today. I wonder why. Am I feeling bad about some other aspect of my life? Am I stressed about work, my relationship or lack of a relationship? Do I feel like I have to look like a model in order to be lovable?" Just ask the questions and see if any answers come. If there are no answers today, let that be OK, too. Embrace where you are now without the need for instant change. *Right now, in this moment, it's all good!*

Remember that your negative thoughts don't have to go anywhere; you just need to add positive thoughts to the mix. Yes, once again, I know the positive mantras might feel silly at first. You might feel uncomfortable saying, "I love my body," because in truth, you don't—not in that moment. But there's value in repeating mantras over and over. You now know that the word *mantra* actually translates to "instrument of the mind," and this instrument is used as a tool of protection. The act of saying the words drives out the negative thoughts without conscious effort on your part. At the same time, you open the door to the possibility of the new thought becoming your truth. By accepting that you might not believe the mantras right away but that there's value in repeating them, you make space for the positive mantras to take hold and become more dominant than your negative thoughts. That sounds good, right?

During your time in meditation, simply begin to entertain the possibility that the negative thoughts about your body are false. That one little thing is all you have to do today. You will build on that—I promise. "I'm learning to love my body just as it is" will eventually become "I love my body just as it is."

Don't forget that you can release the negative thought out loud. "I release the belief that my body isn't good enough. My body *is* good enough." If you really don't believe that last statement today, let yourself laugh. That's OK, too! Remember to fake it until you make it! When the mantras are repeated enough, your behavior and your body will become a natural reflection of your new beliefs. I know many living, breathing examples who have proven this to be true.

Honoring and Respecting Your Body

I'm going to give you another break: you don't have to think your body is beautiful, and you don't have to "love" your body—ever. If the word *love* works for you, use it. If you cringed at the thought of using the word *love,* try honoring, respecting, and accepting your body instead. Eventually you can substitute *love* for those, but only when you feel ready.

As women, our bodies go through so many changes throughout our lives (certainly more than most men). It's an astronomical task to love your body through every stage! Just as I respect my family and friends with all their imperfections, I can *honor and respect* my body without thinking it's beautiful. I can acknowledge what I perceive as imperfections without those imperfections affecting my acceptance of my body.

It just makes sense to me to honor this vessel that gets me where I need to go every day, whether or not I like the way it looks 24/7. This body allows me to live my life, so it deserves some appreciation.

I have found that when I honor my body as it is without focusing on how it looks, my choices reflect that honoring. "Does this plate of food honor me? Does this relationship honor me? Does this decision honor me?" If I answer those questions honestly, and take loving action in response, I can't go wrong.

How on Earth Will Meditation Help Me Lose Weight?

Well, this isn't a weight-loss book; it's a meditation book. The truth is, if you want to lose weight, meditation may or may not help you do it. But I know for certain that weight management is inside job that manifests itself on the outside. We focus so much on the external—counting calories and inches, checking in with our apps, reading books, and trying every new fad diet—that we don't take the time to check in with ourselves. What's going on inside? Weight loss is less about body-punishing workouts and counting calories than about honoring yourself with food and movement choices that nurture you.

No, you don't have to love your body every day, and you don't have to get rid of all those nagging, nasty thoughts. But here's the truth of the matter: you will never maintain a healthy weight unless and until you change your mind-set. Yes, you really do have to move toward accepting your body as it is right now.

Spread the Love

The body I want will not be available to me
unless I do the inside work—period. #YH4M

So it isn't that all those Facebook memes were wrong. They just made you feel like you had to get to your destination without any kind of road map.

Meditation became *my* road map to honoring, respecting, and accepting the body I have. I believe it can do that for you, too, whether you need to lose weight, whether you have an eating disorder that makes it hard to eat at all, or whether you just struggle to be OK with how you look. (Of course, if you're struggling with disordered eating or exercise habits, please seek medical attention immediately!)

The truth is that eating too little or eating too much are really two sides of the same coin. They're both about a lack of control. Many people even flip back and forth between overindulgence and deprivation. When we feel out of control about our weight, we tend to take extreme measures and become obsessive in an effort to regain control. But *real* control comes only through honoring and respecting our bodies and our emotions—even the negative feelings.

I learned this the hard way. I was in a terrible space when I was pregnant with baby number four. I worked out obsessively and compared myself to other pregnant women. "Why am I so much bigger at 30 weeks than that woman over there?" I exercised to the point that I was unable to walk. I became frightened that my pregnancy was ruining my body. It felt like my body was under attack, and I couldn't control what was happening to it. I loved my baby and wanted to care for her, but at the same time, I fought every pound I gained. I had an unhealthy reaction to what was perfectly normal.

I had had a meditation practice before that pregnancy, but I had let it fall by the wayside. As a result, I injured and abused my body. When I returned to my meditation practice, I began to honor my body again with healthy choices.

If you aren't at a healthy weight and you don't have a medical condition that prevents you from losing weight, you have to accept that your actions have led you to this place. But don't use that knowledge as an excuse to beat up on yourself! There's a difference between blaming yourself and taking responsibility for what has prevented you from healthy eating and exercise.

Blame is a judgment that keeps you stuck. Responsibility, on the other hand, empowers you and allows you to take action—to move forward. Responsibility removes the obstacles to your goal because there's nothing outside of you that can stop you from getting what you want. It begins and ends with you, and that can be exciting. Remember: accepting responsibility is a gift and an opportunity.

Again, just allow for the possibility that you can move from blame to responsibility. *Allow!*

CAN YOU HONOR YOUR BODY WITH . . . CAKE?

In 2013 my mother passed away 10 days after a sudden, massive stroke, only seven months after I had lost my father. One day not long after Mom's death, I was standing in a local deli with my 14-year-old son, ready to have a special lunch date—just the two of us.

There in the display case was a Jewish apple cake, something I had never seen in a deli in that part of South New Jersey. Since I had spent that morning and the night before thinking a lot about my mom, I smiled to myself when I saw the cake. Jewish apple cake was one of her few specialties, and she made it often. I took that cake as a sign, maybe even a "hello" from her.

After ordering our sandwiches and potato salad, I gave in to the urging of the Universe and my longing for a taste of my mom's cake. I ordered a slice for each of us and got more excited for it with every bite of my sandwich. I couldn't wait to taste it again. It had been so long.

There's generally not much room for cake or refined sugars of any kind in my diet, but eating that huge piece of cake was in total alignment with my purpose. That cake wasn't meant to cover a pain or fill a void. It wasn't a decadent treat or a cheat on my otherwise pristine diet. That cake was a warm hug. It was a reminder that life's beauty (and my mom) is everywhere. It surprised me in the deli case much like my mother would stop by unannounced with her own cake, still warm from the oven and sprinkled with powdered sugar, ready for us to devour in one sitting.

Sometimes when we ask, "Does this serve and honor me?" and we're asking from a place of genuine love and respect for our purpose, the answer surprises us. More often than not, a yoga class or a giant kale salad will get a resounding YES! Other times we'll get a yes to a piece of cake or playing hooky or watching a marathon of our favorite reality show instead of going to the gym.

Only you can know when you've been truthful with yourself or when you've fooled yourself. If you do fool yourself or find yourself bingeing, remember to look at your behavior with curiosity instead of judgment. "I wonder why I felt the need to binge. Was I stressed out? Was I afraid about something? Did I feel like I'd failed and needed to be punished? Was I just sad?" Whatever the reason, just make note of it for future reference. Allow yourself to say, "That's interesting," as you would about a loved one.

The "Weighting" Game

Meditation is how I keep my mind in shape, but it's far from a quick fix from a physical perspective. While you might feel better in general after a meditation that focuses on your body, you won't see any difference in the mirror—not yet. Meditation is the positive, loving solution to a problem you've dealt with for a long time, so it will take a while to see results. Nevertheless, if you're trying to lose weight, the entire course of that journey can be redirected in *just one* meditation session.

Meditation helps you focus your awareness on self-respect— even on those days when it's the last thing you really feel . . . or maybe *especially* on those days. If you're moving mindlessly through your day, you aren't being careful to honor yourself.

That's why your whole day changes when you start your morning with a meditation—just 4 minutes to self-honor and set a tone for the whole day. It will help you remember throughout the day to ask that important question: "Does this serve me?" Meditation will help you *want* to take good care of your body without counting calories or depriving yourself or avoiding the bakery counter at the grocery store. I have found that honoring my body has become an effortless result of the inner work I do every day.

I'm not saying that meditation has rid me of my problems, but it's a great tool that helps me manage my feelings and stress level. Even when I abandon my practice for a day, I recognize the difference in the way I act, react, and feel.

Just taking the 4 minutes to care enough about yourself to sit down and say, "I release this belief that I'll never love my body," is a step toward self-love—yes, even on the days when the negativity won't let up.

You're on a journey toward relaxing the hold that the negative thoughts have on you, and each day that you meditate, you take another step on that journey. Careful, compassionate mindfulness for just 4 minutes will help you counteract those media images and open your heart—a little bit at a time—to yourself.

Spread the Love

*If I keep my mind in shape, it will help
me keep my body in shape—forever.* #YH4M

Meditation for Body Confidence

Preparation / About This Meditation

"Having the body you want starts with loving the body you have." Before you throw your hands up in the air in defeat, meditate on those words for just a moment. What are they really saying? What do they mean? I once saw a motivational quote on Instagram that really stuck with me: "I don't work out because I hate my body. I work out because I love it." *That* was an aha moment for me. What if accomplishing my goal is about improving an already good situation instead of running from a bad one? What if honoring and respecting the body I'm in right now is the key to *wanting* to take care of this body? And what if, in the process, my body ends up looking better than it ever has?

I wrote this meditation in the spirit of happy beginnings. When you start from a place of honor and respect, it can only be expanded upon with healthy choices.

This is meant to be a meditation of protection, as well as one to increase confidence and power. You will be called upon to express new attitudes and opinions about yourself during your meditation. Remember that repeating these words—even if they feel silly or untrue at first—will begin to make them your own.

When? Do this meditation first thing in the morning or in the early afternoon. It might energize you, so I recommend avoiding it in the evening or before bed. While it isn't designed specifically to increase energy, you could feel a powerful emotional response while repeating the mantras, and that could certainly wake you up.

Where? You can practice this meditation absolutely any-where—in bed first thing in the morning, on your floor pillow, or seated at your desk at the beginning of your workday. Don't concern yourself with making your environment completely dis-traction-free. Because you're repeating mantras, your mind will naturally rid itself of many distractions, both inner and outer.

Position? Place yourself in your Easy Seat.

Your hands, with fingers outstretched, are best upturned on your thighs or knees in Surya Mudra to cultivate warmth and posi-tive energy while you repeat your mantras.

Your eyes may remain open and focused softly on a space or object in front of you. You may choose to keep your eyes closed during the whole meditation, opening them after each cycle of breaths to check in and read the next instruction. Choose what-ever allows you to feel most focused and at ease.

You Have 4 Minutes to Love / Honor / Respect Your Body

Start by focusing your attention on your breath. If you're prac-ticing this meditation first thing in the morning, you may not be fully awake, so be careful not to slump in your seat. Your breath needs a straight and easy path to travel so that it can carry energy throughout your entire body. Soon you'll begin to attract positive energy from all around you with your thoughts and spoken man-tras. Create a clear path for that energy to flow.

The mantras below are an offering to your heart—a gift from you to you. They're an affirmation of your strength, purpose, and beauty. Choose one of the three mantras (or any individual sen-tence from each mantra) for today's practice.

1. Without manipulating your breath, observe how it feels in your chest—your heart center. Feel your lungs

fill with air, warmed by your body. Feel your chest fill and lift with this warm air. Observe how filling your chest as completely as you can causes you to sit up even taller in your seat. As you exhale slowly, feel your lungs empty and the air pass through your throat and out through your mouth or nostrils.

2. If you've chosen to keep your eyes open, it's time to close them for just a bit if you can. Continue this chest breathing with your eyes closed for ten cycles of inhales and exhales. Observe how your breaths deepen and lengthen during this time. At the end of your breath cycles, open your eyes for your next instruction.

3. Your posture has attracted positive energy. You're sitting up tall, and you appear confident and strong. Even though you're fully relaxed, your mouth has revealed a tiny smile. Your shoulders are rolled back and down, leaving your chest open wide to the space in front of you. Your whole body appears to be smiling. Your open chest is a portal for positive energy to enter your body on the inhale and return to the outside world on the exhale.

4. Your deep, long, and smooth breaths will continue to warm your body and fill you with energy. As this energy flows to every part of you, warming your arms to your fingertips and your legs to your toes, imagine the warmth as light. Imagine your body filling with light until you become a glowing, radiant being.

5. For the mantra portion of this meditation, you'll continue to breathe as you have been for seven additional full cycles: Inhale fully, filling your chest with energizing, warming air. As you exhale, repeat your chosen mantra.

Mantra 1

I think loving thoughts about my body. I am compassionate toward my body. I am always mindful of my thoughts. My body hears my thoughts and responds well when I'm loving to myself. My thoughts about my body are forgiving and kind.

Mantra 2

My words are gentle. I speak gently about myself to myself and to others. I use words like "beautiful," "strong," and "healthy" to describe my body. I choose the words. No one may speak poorly about my body.

Mantra 3

I am strong. I am healthy. I am powerful. I am filled with radiant energy. I am a vision of beauty and confidence to all who see me. My body serves me well, and I am grateful for it. My body is a beautiful, miraculous machine and a sacred vessel for my soul.

The Meditation Continues . . .

1. Your mantra has taken root, and your heart has already started to believe its truth. As you move through your day and interact with family, friends, and strangers, they will see what you've already begun to believe. You're sitting up taller now, and you're radiating positive energy. If you could see your energy, it would look like warm light—a glowing, yellow light originating in your belly. Close your eyes for just a few breaths—two or three cycles of long inhales and exhales that fill your chest—and imagine yourself completely absorbed by the light. Imagine your yellow-orange light swirling and churning

around you as if on the surface of the sun. You are a brilliant sun in the middle of your universe.

2. You will recall this sun image throughout your day, and it will lift you energetically and physically. You'll stand taller, walk more purposefully, and feel warmed by this protective shield of vibrant light. It will attract all the energy you need to continue to carry yourself with confidence. You feel powerful and purposeful, but above all else, beautiful inside and out.

Meditation for Weight Loss

Preparation / About This Meditation

If you're reading this meditation, you're probably trying to lose weight or maintain prior weight loss. Losing weight may be one of the most stressful and daunting physical efforts you ever attempt, so it's my hope that this meditation will create a space of ease and comfort for you.

You're not alone if workouts sometimes leave you feeling defeated or if hopelessness follows your every new attempt at dieting. You've been promised the body of your dreams time and time again, but in the end, you're still trapped in a body that just won't shrink. You're constantly battling your weight, you've made food the enemy, and your spirit has become a tragic casualty. This meditation can heal all that has been wounded in this fight. You can shrink your waistline and your worry in just 4 minutes.

When? You may practice this meditation at any time, and it's actually most useful practiced in shorter form many times throughout the day.

Where? Pick a quiet space for this meditation. You'll be prompted to ask yourself questions, and it's important that outside distractions don't interfere with your ability to hear the answers. They may come in the form of an inner voice, a feeling, or an image. Be patient! During my time in meditation, I sometimes see words on a page. I call this my "inner instruction manual." Other times I visualize a teacher in a classroom setting. My good friend and personal hypnotherapist, Grace Smith, taught a version of this meditation to me once during a hypnosis session. I ask the "teacher" questions, and she answers honestly and objectively. In reality, the teacher is just my inner voice, free from distraction or judgment, but picturing her as someone separate from me allows me to act out the question and more easily answer. Visualizations and "play-acting" can be powerful tools for your own meditation practice.

Position? Sit in your Easy Seat.

Because you're calling on your intuition for answers during this meditation, you may want to place your hands on your thighs or knees with your hands and fingers in the Gyan Mudra position.

Follow the instructions within the meditation for opening and closing your eyes.

You Have 4 Minutes for Weight Loss

1. Sitting up nice and tall, with your eyes still open and focused softly on a single space or object in front of you, start to bring attention to your breath. Be careful to allow your breath to flow in and out with ease. Don't try to change it. If you're restless, your breath might become quick and audible, so try not to create any unnecessary noise with your breath. Allow it to slow down. The point of this exercise is to make your environment as quiet as possible.

2. After you've quieted your breath, it will soon be time to close your eyes, if you can, in order to remove all visual distractions from your meditation space. Check in after each section or cycle of breaths for further instruction.

Visualize Your Classroom . . .

3. Begin to imagine objects from a classroom. Desks, chairs, and a blackboard will soon appear around you. The classroom is warm and cheerful with colorful decorations and big windows that look out to a beautiful landscape.

4. Picture a teacher standing in front of the classroom. Your teacher has a friendly and inviting face, and you feel completely comfortable in his/her presence. From this point on, all your questions will be directed toward your teacher, and answers will be returned swiftly. Every answer will be true and will be in complete service of your mission to become healthier, happier, and stronger.

5. With your eyes focused on your chosen object, or gently closed, direct each of the following questions to your teacher, either silently or aloud, and wait for the answer to come to you. Once you have your answers, read your next step.

   "How may I eat today to honor my body, my mission, and my heart?"

   "How may I move today to honor my body, my mission, and my heart?"

   "How may I speak today to honor my body, my mission, and my heart?"

6. You'll receive your answers immediately. Your teacher—your inner voice—will tell you exactly what to do to honor yourself today. The instructions will be easy for you to carry out, and you'll see no obstacles between you and doing all you can to treat your body and your spirit well.

7. After you've received your answers and have accepted them into your heart as the absolute truth, seal your meditation with ten more breaths. With every

inhale, you feel more joyful and determined. With every exhale, you release any remaining worry about making healthy choices.

For the remainder of the day, you can reactivate this meditation by taking three full breaths and asking yourself one question: "How does this honor my body, my mission, and my heart?"

Ask this question before every meal or snack, before entering a potentially stressful exchange with another person, or before making the choice between the elevator and the stairs. Frequently throughout your day, take a moment to slow down and check in. When you're completely honest with yourself in these times of quiet, careful contemplation, your answers may surprise you as often as they are completely predictable. Like I've said before, sometimes a brownie can honor you as well as a yoga class. Receive each answer to your question in the spirit of nonjudgment, know that the answer is true and in service of you, and enjoy the nourishing moments that follow.

Meditation for Body Acceptance

Preparation / About This Meditation

In your Meditation for Body Confidence, I asked you to repeat mantras that may not necessarily be true for you in the moment. These little fibs that you tell yourself during meditation are actually just glimpses—predictions—of what can and *will* be true for you in the future. Through constant repetition, what once felt impossible will slowly become believable. And once you believe something, you'll begin to see it in your life for real. I know this may sound a little "woo-woo" to a lot of you, but this is one of the principle rules of manifesting. Imagine what you could do if you truly believed that nothing could get in your way.

Body Confidence teaches you to be gentle and kind to your body. This meditation teaches you to be gentle and kind to your *feelings* about your body. What does that mean? You now have permission to feel not-so-nice feelings, to feel no guilt about not loving what you see in the mirror, and to finally have a "fat day" without feeling like you're letting down all womankind. A practice of acceptance of both your body (in all its changing shapes and stages) and your thoughts about your body will allow you to move closer to your goals. You'll no longer be the obstacle getting in the way of your own progress because you won't waste time fighting your own feelings or shaming yourself for having them.

You may notice that I use the words *not love* in place of *hate* during this meditation. A lot of you might hate your body, and I told you earlier in the chapter that it's OK to feel that way. But during your time in meditation, your goal should be to reframe both the thoughts and the words you use to talk about yourself. Even during a practice of accepting nonpositive feelings, I think it's important to use gentle words. You may feel like you *hate* your body (or parts of it) today, but how can you change your words during meditation to be more compassionate toward your body and your feelings about your body?

Meditation may still be new to you, but soon you'll be able to create your own meditations. As you move forward with your personal practice, please consider these inspirations for meditations on body acceptance:

- I allow all thoughts—whether so-called good or bad—but I speak only words that are loving and kind. I will think lovingly about myself. I will be compassionate toward myself. I will think loving words. I will look at my reflection and give thanks for this beautiful, miraculous machine that has been gifted to me.

- Are my words kind? How do I speak about myself to myself and to others? What words do I allow in my vocabulary in reference to my body? These words are negative: fat, weak, ugly. These words are positive: beautiful, strong, healthy. I will speak in loving terms about my body.

This meditation is a sort of supplement to Body Confidence. All those positive thoughts and words in that meditation are pure, clean nourishment for your journey. But like a food diet, where a craving for a cupcake sometimes wins over a green smoothie, there will be days when the negativity just won't be squashed by positive thoughts. Vitamin supplements fill the holes in your *almost* perfect diet, and this meditation supplement will help balance your *almost* perfect positive-thinking practice.

When? This meditation is appropriate for any time of the day, so practice it when you need it most.

Where? I always prefer that you practice your meditations in places that allow for the greatest amount of comfort. If you're feeling physically uncomfortable, meditation can be difficult, and feeling self-conscious about being heard or seen while you meditate can be particularly unsettling. This meditation may bring up a lot of intense feelings, so be sure you're in a space that allows you to let go of your innermost vulnerabilities without fear or apprehension. Your bedroom may be the perfect spot. Climb into bed, surrounded by your favorite pillows and blankets, and prepare yourself for meditation.

Position? Find a seated position that's most comfortable for you and allows your chest to remain open with ease. If an open-heart posture is difficult for you to maintain while sitting up without back support, a reclined position may be a better choice. If this is your preference, refer to Chapter 2 for instructions on Semireclined Bound Angle Pose or Corpse Pose with bent knees. These reclining postures are perfect for a practice of acceptance and surrender.

As illustrated in the posture instructions, your arms will be lying beside you, with palms turned upward and fingers outstretched. If you're sitting up, place your hands upturned on your thighs or knees.

I recommend that you practice this one with your eyes closed if you can. After each section of instruction, gently open your eyes to read and receive your next set of cues.

You Have 4 Minutes to *Not* Love Your Body

Feeling not so great about how you look or how your body is serving you can cause anxiety, as well as depression. These feelings can drag on, come and go, or switch from one to the other. Honor where you are in this moment by taking just a little bit of time to check in. This time doesn't need to be longer than the duration of a few breaths.

1. With your eyes closed (or open and softly focused), and your body resting comfortably in your chosen seat, place your attention on your breath and its characteristics in this moment. Count five inhales and exhales while observing the length, depth, and smoothness of each breath. Your breath may be short or long, shallow or deep, rattled or smooth. None of these characteristics are better or more correct than the others. Your job in this moment is to observe, not to judge.

2. As you continue to breathe, recall the biggest thing that's bothering you about your body (or your behaviors relating to your body) right now. What brought you to this meditation today? You may feel embarrassed about your answer because you think being unhappy with a part of yourself is a sign of failure. Let's release that right now.

3.   Inhale as deeply as you can, feeling the air fill your chest and then your belly until it's big and round. As you exhale, allow every muscle in your body to release and to feel as though it's melting into the surface beneath you.

4.   Inhale once more. Exhale, and say aloud (or silently if you're in a public place), "I release the idea that it's wrong to not love everything about my body all the time." Alternatively you might say, "I release the idea that I have to love everything about my body all the time."

5.   Continue to repeat this mantra four more times for a total of five times. If it feels unnatural, even after the fifth repetition, you can continue for 21 total breath cycles. There's no need to move on to the next mantra—save it for another time. But if you're ready to move on to the next step, let's set up your personal mantra for today.

6.   Fill in the blanks in the following mantra with the appropriate body part or body-related behavior that you're struggling with: "I accept that I do not love my _____ today. I release the idea that my thoughts about my _____ have to be positive all the time."

7.   Continue your pattern of deep, body-filling inhales and long, muscle-relaxing exhales for five full breath cycles. Repeat your personal mantra on each exhale. The words of release with each exhale allow your body to sink deeper into relaxation, melting you even further into the floor beneath you.

8.   Fill in the blank for your final mantra: "I can be unhappy with my _____ and still love and accept my body." Repeat your second personal mantra on each exhale for five more full breath cycles.

These are your personal mantras of love, acceptance, and release. They are your protection from self-defeating thoughts that get in the way of your progress. They may teach you to accept your nonpositive thoughts about your body but they also teach you how to love (honor) your body as it is in this moment. *Loving (honoring) the body you have allows you to have the body you want.*

Bonus "Moving" Meditation for When Cravings Strike

With regard to self-esteem, grief, or any other topic covered in this book, there's a way to avoid the main triggers that cause distress. With food, though, you're constantly confronted by your triggers. You have to eat, and food is everywhere. So how can you live normally when stumbling blocks are in front of you several times a day, every day?

Sitting down in lotus position in the middle of a busy café probably isn't the best way to contemplate whether or not the chocolate croissant calling to you from the display case is a good idea. You might have heard of the concept of taking your yoga off the mat and into the world. I want you to take your meditation off the pillow, and I'll show you how to do that in this bonus "moving" meditation—which can be practiced on the go with a set of mantras in the form of questions and affirmations to help you make loving decisions about food throughout your day.

The result from this type of meditation is instant. You ask the question, your earlier pillow work is recalled, and you make the perfect eating-related decision for that moment. You might struggle with the answers at first—mostly over how truthful they are—but they will come. How well the answers serve you will change with time. There will be times that the truth comes swiftly and without effort, and there will be whole chunks of time when you're giving yourself the green light to foods that would be better left alone. This practice is as much one of self-examination as it is one of self-love. You have to constantly check in with yourself to make sure you're being truthful.

Mindfulness about how you eat is the foundation for maintaining healthy eating habits. When you take the time to think about how each of your eating-related decisions serves you *before* you take that first bite, you'll naturally eat more appropriately and begin to lose weight.

Eventually all your eating-related decisions will become easy. The questions will come automatically; you won't even notice you've asked them. The answers will appear as pure knowing with no waiting time whatsoever. Constant, intentional practice becomes habit, and your choices about eating will be completely intuitive.

Moving Meditation

1. Take a breath before you taste to avoid making a
    decision in haste. Then ask:

    > How does this [food] serve me?
    > How will I feel after I eat this [food]?

2. Affirm what is true—your eating decisions should be
    worthy of you:

    > I will eat foods that bring me pleasure. I will eat
    > without regret or judgment.
    > I live actively and eat real food.
    > The body I have is the one I'm meant to have . . .
    > and it's beautiful!
    > Junk food is for junk bodies. I treat my body
    > like a temple.
    > What I choose to nourish my body is a clear
    > indication of how much I love myself. I eat with
    > self-respect.
    > When I come from a place of self-love and
    > not from denial or punishment, all eating-related
    > decisions become effortless and worthy of me.
    > I treat myself by making loving food choices.

Bon appétit!

Chapter 6

4 Minutes to Discover True Happiness

For a long time, I believed there had been no joyful moments in my childhood. I looked back and saw it as 100 percent miserable, and I even thought that misery was my destiny. Then I was able to set that aside and realize that happiness was something I could achieve in spite of my childhood. But that mind-set still made it necessary for me to "overcome" my past in order to be happy.

Then a single meditation experience changed everything for me.

In meditation I asked myself this question: "When was I content in my childhood?" After meditating on the word *content* for a good amount of time and focusing on the true definition according to my heart, I was instantly flooded with all sorts of images. Among them was a memory that altered my perspective about happiness forever—a memory of what had always been a very traumatic and defining event in my life.

When I was a kid, my dad often collected aluminum cans to take to the recycling center in exchange for money to help pay our bills. I was about seven years old, and my younger sister was about four, and we wanted very much to buy something. Instead of buying us whatever we wanted, our dad took us can collecting with him. He took us to flea markets and public spaces and down to the train tracks where the teenagers hung out and threw their beer cans on the ground or in the garbage. We were just like the homeless people who collect cans out of the trash. We got filthy as we gathered the sticky, smelly cans, and we were left covered in ticks when we collected in the woods.

When I think about how it must have looked to other people, my first reaction is to cringe a little bit. And when I became a mother, it became even harder for me to understand how my mom let our dad do it. For so many years, I looked back on that experience with shame, disgust, and anger.

In meditation, though, I remembered a particular day when we were collecting on the train tracks. In my mind, I could vividly see myself with my sister and father going into the woods. I could see the alcove where the teenagers would hang out. I could see their burned-out bonfire. I could see the cans scattered all around it. I saw those Old Milwaukee cans—the white ones with the red labels. It was all so vivid.

But the feelings that came up during my meditation didn't match my usual feeling of humiliation. I didn't feel disgust at all. When I tuned into my child self, I was surprised to discover that what I felt was excitement. Outside of meditation, I never would have been able to recall that feeling. I had to really go back into my memory.

I saw myself quickly gathering the cans and crushing them like my dad had taught me. This made more room in my garbage bag so that I could collect even more cans. I saw something like a halo of light around each can, and they were sparkling. Everything was vibrant. The leaves on the ground and the trees were almost electric green.

Why was I so excited back then? As I collected my many cans, I thought, "I can buy so many My Little Pony toys with these!"

In my meditation I saw myself running toward my dad and sister to tell them how many cans I had gathered. I wasn't this dirty little kid being carried around by my hapless father who couldn't make enough money to take care of his family. Suddenly I was an adventurer, a pirate finding treasure. To my child self, it was actually romantic.

When I came out of that meditation, I realized that I'd been angry with my father for years for something that had actually been a joyful experience for me. I learned in that moment that happiness is often a matter of perspective. We place intellectual demands on our lives that specify what happiness can and cannot be instead of paying attention to how we truly feel in the moment. Sometimes the demands we place on our definition of happiness are based on what we believe other people would think. We can't be happy until we're rich enough to have as much as our neighbors or as good a marriage as our sister or brother.

Often we don't even know what would truly make us happy. We have ideas about it that may or may not have anything to do with reality. No wonder happiness eludes so many of us.

Meditation allows us to extract the opinions of others from the dialogue. It even allows us to extract our own opinions from the dialogue, as it did in my case. In meditation we can go into the center of what being happy really means to us on a deep level.

Most of the time in our lives, we're seen or heard or read by others—in person, on the phone, or on social media. The great thing about meditating is that we can just be silent observers of ourselves. We can ask questions like "How do I really feel?"

FEELINGS ARE LIKE BREEZES

When you ask yourself how you feel, remind yourself not to answer, "I'm sad," or "I'm happy." You feel sad. You aren't sadness. The same is true of happiness. Our feelings are like breezes. One passes through us, and then a new breeze passes. This process of feelings coming and going and coming again is constant and predictable, even if we can't predict exactly what those feelings are going to be.

> Just like total peace or unwavering self-love, it isn't realistic to expect pure happiness to be a static state that we achieve 24/7. Nobody manages that in life. But we do have the capacity to allow more happy moments in our lives. When we string them together, we can experience a life filled with happiness.

Happiness = Contentment

Therapists have asked me, "What are your happiest moments from childhood?" As I said, I was always hard-pressed to think of any. One of the main reasons for that block is that I equated happiness with joy. I don't think I'm alone in that misconception.

Many of us believe that happiness has to be a heightened moment of jumping up and down with unbridled excitement. The truth is that during my childhood, I didn't really have many moments like that, at least not when it came to my home life. The experience of collecting cans with my father and sister is as close as I got to that kind of joy. But as I've expanded my idea of what happiness means, I've been able to look back and see that there were many times in my childhood when I was *content* and *satisfied*.

When we put happiness in the same box as joy, it feels like such an effort. It's exaggerated, demonstrative, and actually a bit exhausting. Think about it: Would you want to be in a heightened state of joy all the time? Would you want to be around a person who was in a heightened state of joy all the time? If you've ever met someone like that, didn't you feel that something was "off" and not quite healthy about him or her?

That's because most of the time, happiness is quieter and simpler than that. It's about being able to sit with your eyes open, see all that you have, and feel ease, knowing that in that moment, you have what you need. When we're open to happiness in our day-to-day lives, we actually open ourselves up to the possibility of experiencing more moments of heightened joy and ecstasy.

Here's how I see it: Joy is like jumping up and down on a trampoline. Happiness is sitting next to the trampoline as I watch my children jump up and down. That's an effortless kind of happiness. Sure, I like to hop onto the trampoline, but I also like to hop off when I need a break. That doesn't mean my happiness ends. Even in the moments when I'm feeling down, I can usually find happiness around me and allow it in. I don't have to participate in it directly. I can find it in the laughter of a baby or the beauty of a bird or being surprised by my favorite song on the radio. I can even find it in a cat video on YouTube.

When I went into meditation and asked for memories of contentment in my childhood—rather than asking for memories of joy—I remembered another time when I was collecting worms in my backyard with my neighbor. This was a regular activity—worm-collecting contests. I'd fill an entire McDonald's Happy Meal bucket with the worms, and we'd go fishing at the creek together. It was so ordinary that I wouldn't have even recalled it in answer to a question about my "happiest" moments from childhood. I had never thought of such ordinary moments as "happy." But when I shifted my thinking to "contentment," the memory was waiting for me, and I could see that it really had been a happy moment after all. I just needed to realize that happiness was not only about the spectacular.

Then, when I expanded my point of view beyond home, where I experienced most of my traumas as a kid, I found countless "happy" memories. I opened myself up to reexperience magical Christmases and summer visits to the Jersey Shore with my aunt Kathy, epic backyard adventures with neighborhood kids, and the feeling of pride when I won awards for my artwork in high school. "Finding the happy" required paying close attention and sorting through some of the painful memories that were taking up more than their fair share of space. It took traveling back in time to experience the reality of each moment, not just my later opinions about them, to reveal the happy stuff.

Recently I shared a simple but truly happy moment with my husband. We were outside when we happened to notice two dung beetles rolling a little ball of poop. I had thought dung beetles lived only in Africa. I didn't know they were also in the U.S., much less New Jersey! It was literally a tiny source of happiness for us. My husband even made a video of them and put it up on Instagram—a way of spreading the good feelings.

Our happiness at watching those dung beetles was sparked by curiosity and discovery. When we're kids, it's innate to find happiness in curiosity and discovery, but we tend to lose this ability when we reach adulthood. All we have to do is notice that there is beauty all around us and happiness taking place all the time. All we have to do is look up, look down, and look around. Even though meditation is a practice of going inside, it has also helped me get out of my own head enough that when I open my eyes and go about my day, I notice more of the happiness that's available to me—literally right in my own backyard!

It may sound like a cliché to see the beauty in the little things, but it's an important truth. And it's a truth that we tend to forget as we become caught up in the seemingly endless problems that we have to solve on a daily basis.

Even though I lived in poverty as a child, had witnessed abuse, and was the victim of neglect, there were many moments in my life when I connected with the simple things and felt content. My natural state was still happiness—just by virtue of being a curious child who could see the beauty in collecting worms.

So just as I learned that calm can be experienced in the middle of chaos, I also discovered that happiness can be experienced even in the midst of a great deal of misery. I don't think we can survive if there aren't some moments of happiness. Don't get me wrong: I would never diminish the real pain that people experience. But we're often blind to the fact that happiness is available to us if we just let it in. And when we do let it in, it's exactly what makes it possible for us to cope. Have you ever had a funny thought and busted out in laughter in the middle of crying or during an extremely uncomfortable moment? In these cases, laughter is our saving grace. The more we learn to allow those moments in, the better we'll get through the rough times and truly enjoy the good times.

Happiness Doesn't Require Perfection

That brings me to my next point about what keeps many of us from experiencing the happiness that's right in front of us—the belief that we can't be happy until everything is perfect. Is happiness the picket fence, the loving relationship with the perfect partner, the 2.5 kids, and the job with the high salary? Perfection is an ideal that we can never achieve. Just as we can't postpone peace until our lives are stress-free, if we put happiness on hold until we reach perfection, we'll never experience it.

Have you ever seen the television reality show *Bridezillas?* In it, the brides go ballistic at the slightest hint that something might go wrong on their wedding day. Weddings are also a great metaphor for life. Just as there's no such thing as a perfect life, there's no such thing as a perfect wedding. If we can't experience happiness on that day without perfection, our marriages will be doomed before they even start.

I already mentioned that my husband forgot to bring the video camera to our wedding. We had decided not to hire a videographer but just have a friend do it for us. And it was my groom's job to bring the camera. Talk about an opportunity to turn into a bridezilla! I could have let that make me crazy and completely ruin my wedding. But I *chose* to let it go. I still have the memory of our beautiful day in my mind, even if I don't have a video record of it.

It's simply a waste of time to try to make things perfect. (Of course, I've had to remind myself of that many times while writing this book!) In my meditation practice—to maintain my general mental and emotional health—I make it a point to remember that my life doesn't have to be perfect to be working. It doesn't have to be perfect to make me feel good. It just needs to be good enough so that I can feel peaceful and supported as I work toward my goals. And while I don't find that kind of support every single day, I can have it *almost* every day if I remove the requirements of perfection and heightened joy. Remember: happiness is not found only in perfection.

Spread the Love

When I release the idea that everything has to be perfect before I can be happy, it's easy to find happiness in the here and now.
#YH4M

You Are the Source

One of my favorite quotes is "I still remember a time when I wished for what I have now." When I first read it, that quote told me, like a smack to the face, to appreciate the here and now and stop complaining so much. As I think you know about me by now, I'm not one of those people who will tell you it's unsafe to *ever* complain. But let's face it—we all do it too much. It's so in our natures to focus on the negative or look for what we need to fix. We think, "If I could just _____, I'd be happy." Fill in the blank with whatever you've told yourself.

If we base our happiness on things that are changeable, our ability to be happy teeters on a razor's edge, ready to drop us into unhappiness at any moment. If you can't be happy unless you're married, what happens if your marriage ends for some reason? If you can't be happy unless you have a particular job, what happens if you don't get that job? There are people in dire circumstances who still manage to be happy or at least have moments of contentment, regardless of what they endure. We can all learn a lot from them.

We have to find a way to *be* our happiness. Rather than *seek* happiness, we can learn to cultivate it within ourselves. Yes, we allow external things to bring us moments of happiness. We enjoy our marriage as fully as we possibly can, for example, but we're much better off if we don't rely on it for our happiness.

For example, ask yourself: If I separate myself from the idea that I don't have enough money right now, how do I feel? If I separate myself from the fact that somebody doesn't like me, how do I feel? Can I feel contentment even if these so-called negative circumstances remain true?

It helps, of course, to stay in the moment. When we start thinking about the future, worry sets in, and all the thoughts of "What if I can't make the rent?" or "What if I end up alone?" start to plague us and rob us of happiness. Since we don't know what the future will bring, "what if" questions are a pointless exercise. As we've often heard it said, the moment of now is all we have. Experiencing happiness is really a matter of just making the most of each moment.

Spread the Love

Don't SEEK happiness; SEE happiness. When I pay attention, I can see happiness everywhere! #YH4M

That's the challenge—seeing it in the ordinary and the everyday.

In the mantras later in this chapter, I say, "I don't seek the light—I am the light. I drown out all darkness. I'm immune to negativity." We are the light and the happiness that we seek. The painful stuff that happens in our lives is the darkness, but the light within us can allow us to feel happiness even in the midst of darkness. No matter what happens to us, we are still the light. Our natural state—before we fell under the influence of other people's opinions, irrational fears, and arbitrary social rules—is lightness, curiosity, discovery, awe, and, yes, happiness. Just as we are *not* our feelings that pass through like breezes, we are *not* the darkness that sometimes comes into our lives. Nothing that happens to us can dim our light. And remember: there is light available to us even at night. The moon and the stars never go out. Let their light be a reminder that our light never goes out either. That source of happiness is always shining . . . if we just look.

Every day there will be opportunities to be happy and opportunities to be unhappy. Which opportunities are you going to say yes to?

I'm not saying that you shouldn't feel pain and grief and loss when they come into your life. Those feelings must be felt and cannot be ignored. But so often what we experience as unhappiness is really just a dull sense of dissatisfaction. In those moments we can make the choice to cultivate openness within ourselves and allow happiness to come, whether it's generated from our own state of being or from something in our external world—a hug, a song, or a slice of Jewish apple cake.

Meditation for Reframing Shame

Preparation / About This Meditation

I had defined myself by a story that turned out to be a lie. And the more I have shared this story and the process of discovering the truth behind it, the more people I've found who've done the same thing.

Collecting cans with my dad didn't bring me shame. The story I've been telling myself about it did. When I took the time to sit in quiet contemplation and examine that time with him without any judgment, I discovered something truly beautiful—a happy memory. Meditation allowed me to travel in time and shed 30 years of untruths that had been attached to my happy event.

You may be dealing with a truly traumatizing event that can't be made positive with meditation. It happened, it sucked, and you don't have to believe anything different. I would never attempt to take away your right to hurt, mourn, or be angry. What I want is for you to be able to see everything that brings you shame for what it truly is—an event or circumstance that is completely disconnected from who you are. You are a radiant being of light blessed with your creator's infinite love. Yes, you are exactly that.

This meditation is one from my personal practice. It's helped me to realize that I've claimed too much ownership for stuff that just isn't mine—including others' opinions. I've accepted blame for too much and carried shame for other people's actions for too long. What regret, shame, or guilt are you carrying for an event or circumstance that you didn't create and had no power to control? Maybe you're like me and you're holding on to opinions about something that could possibly change when the event is examined from a different perspective. Once you have your answer, get ready to start your meditation.

When? Practice this meditation at any time of the day. This is a very special meditation that may stir up old emotions, so it may be a good idea to allow for some time after the meditation to process what happened instead of jumping back into your regular routine right away.

Where? Make sure your meditation space is private and free of distraction. I'm going to guide you to read your mantras out loud, so this may be a meditation to save for a time when you're alone.

Position? Sit in Easy Seat with your hands in Gyan Mudra or with your palms upturned and resting on your thighs or knees.

You'll start with your eyes open, and I'll direct you when to open and close your eyes during your meditation.

You Have 4 Minutes to Change Your Perspective

Start this meditation in Easy Seat—sitting up tall with strong, sturdy posture and feeling fully connected to the surface beneath you. Keep your eyes open for the first part of your practice as you read the following mantras out loud.

1. Inhale all the way down to your seat, and exhale completely between each mantra, allowing yourself to fully absorb the meaning and power of every word.

Mantra 1

I am not defined by anything outside of me.
My body, my job, my relationships, my past . . .
none of these define who I am.

Mantra 2

All the events of my life—past and present—are in service of my spiritual growth and my journey to happiness.

Mantra 3

I accept myself as I am now—flawed in circumstance but perfect in spirit.

2. Take a few moments to examine how you're feeling right now. What came up for you while you were reading those words? Did you experience any physical sensations? Close your eyes for five breath cycles and examine any reactions with curiosity. Then open your eyes and repeat all three mantras out loud without stopping in between: "I am not defined by anything outside of me. My body, my job, my relationships, my past . . . none of these define who I am. All the events of my life—past and present—are in service of my spiritual growth and my journey to happiness. I accept myself as I am now—flawed in circumstance but perfect in spirit."

3. Now it's time to recall the answer to the question I asked before you started this meditation: "What negative feelings are you carrying about an event

or circumstance that you didn't create and had no power to control? Can you look at a negative experience from a new perspective—free of judgment?" This is what you'll contemplate for the rest of this meditation. You may feel uncomfortable—maybe even afraid. If your feelings start to become intense, remind yourself that you're OK, saying out loud, "I'm safe. I'm calm. I choose to be here."

4. When you revisit your event, examine every part of the scene—the environment, the sounds, and the smells. Recall how you felt both physically and emotionally.

5. You have created a strong foundation of protection with the mantras you read out loud at the beginning of this meditation. You're safe to revisit your scene. Allow yourself to imagine your scene with a new perspective, knowing that you're separate from the event.

6. Close your eyes (or soften the focus of your vision with eyes open) and imagine your scene from the safety and comfort of your meditation space. When you feel ready, open your eyes, take three deep breaths, and return to your day.

Meditation for Opening Your Heart

Preparation / About This Meditation

Can we just reenact the "Open Your Heart" music video by Madonna and make this a dance party meditation? There's something about Googling an old hit from childhood, playing the music video, and dancing like no one is watching. Talk about a joyful release! If the song is already playing in your head, you're welcome. If you have no idea what I'm talking about, take a break as soon as you're finished meditating and check out the music video on YouTube. 1986 was a very good year for Madonna.

In the same way that a Madonna dance party is available to you at any time (thank you, Internet!), happiness is right at your fingertips, too. You just have to be open enough to see it! Remember: happiness doesn't have to mean jumping up and down on the trampoline. Happiness is easy and familiar, and within your reach.

The mantras in this meditation will remind you that true happiness is linked to your outlook, not to outside circumstances that can change from moment to moment. When your foundation is built upon a deep knowing that happiness is your natural state and can be accessed at any time, there's no storm you can't weather. You're a brick house, baby!

When? Start your day with this meditation to set yourself on course for seeing the happy everywhere. Birds' songs will sound sweeter, the sun will shine brighter, and every stranger you meet will have a smile for you in return. And if the weather isn't cooperating, you'll see beauty in gray skies, the sounds of raindrops, or whistling winds.

Where? Practice in your favorite meditation spot. Or maybe you'd like to try a meditation in nature. Being outdoors always allows me to more easily see the happy. If it's warm outside, practice in your bare feet. Allowing your skin to come in contact with the earth is a wonderful grounding practice that connects you with the energetic vibrations of the planet. Meditating by a window on a rainy day is another one of my favorite ways to practice.

Position? Settle into Easy Seat with your hands resting gently on your thighs or knees and your palms upturned. Easy Seat should always feel comfortable, but I also want you to remember to sit up nice and tall. Recall the cue to imagine that you're being pulled up toward the sky by an invisible string attached to the crown of your head.

If you can, practice your meditation with your eyes closed when directed. And just for fun, you might want to experiment with smiling during your meditation—especially when repeating your mantras.

You Have 4 Minutes to See the Happy

You already have so many reasons to be happy. Take a moment to examine what's happening right now. You're breathing! Every breath is proof that you're alive and well. You can read! Your potential for learning and growth is unlimited. It's easy to see the happy. The opportunities for happiness are everywhere.

1. Begin your meditation by focusing your attention on your wonderful, full, life-giving inhales and exhales. Feel each breath enter your nostrils, fill your entire body with vibrant energy, and exit through your mouth. You are more energized with each breath.

2. Close your eyes (or soften the focus of your vision) and continue paying attention to your breath until it's smooth and even. When you feel ready, open your eyes to read your first mantra.

3. Close your eyes again and repeat each mantra on your exhale for five full breath cycles. Recite the words with intention, feeling your body absorb the positive energy of your words. Feel the corners of your mouth turn up and take the shape of a smile. Feeling happy is easy in this moment. Open your eyes after each mantra to read your next instruction.

Mantra 1

Today I will look for the good, and the good will find me.

Mantra 2

My eyes and heart are open to the happiness all around me.

Your day has been infused with positivity and light. Your mantras have lifted your spirit and inspired you to see the happy everywhere. You are in total control of how much happiness you welcome into your life today.

4. Revisit your breath for a few moments. Notice how you're breathing deeper, and the positive energy is flowing easily through your entire body. Remember this feeling throughout the day whenever you need a little pick-me-up. Happiness is always within easy reach.

Meditation for Happiness

Preparation / About This Meditation

"If we could change ourselves, the tendencies in the world would also change. As a man changes his own nature, so does the attitude of the world change towards him. This is the divine mystery supreme. A wonderful thing it is and the source of our happiness . . ." —Mahatma Gandhi

Changing your environment is as simple as changing your outlook. Inspiring other people to do the same is as easy as shining your light and allowing them to step into its glow. When you've touched one person's heart, you've changed the whole world forever.

This meditation, inspired by a *metta* meditation (for loving kindness) taught to me by renowned meditation guide davidji, will wake you up to the light that's already inside you and help you shine that light on the world. Recalling your meditation at other times of the day will remind you to turn on your light for others to see. Imagine yourself as a streetlight on a dark night. You're not just the light that shines—you're also lighting up everything around you. Once someone steps into your light, the darkness that surrounds him or her disappears, too.

When? Morning is a perfect time to start spreading light. You'll be able to send light, love, and happiness to others even from your meditation pillow. You might also like trying this meditation whenever you feel like the people around you may need a little happiness pick-me-up.

Where? Of course, it's always nice to meditate in a quiet spot, but I've used this meditation in all sorts of places—in my dressing room on the set of my TV show, in the back of taxis, and in my doctor's waiting room. Use it before a big interview to soften your interviewer or to help ease the nerves of your fellow passengers on the runway before your plane takes off. You are a powerful light-worker doing your magic everywhere!

Position? Energy flows most easily when you're sitting up tall. Sit in Easy Seat with your hands resting on your thighs or knees and your palms upturned. It might feel good to place your hands over your heart center for all or part of your meditation.

I'm going to guide you through a visualization of your Heart Chakra, so it's best if you can close your eyes during parts of this meditation.

You Have 4 Minutes to Spread Happiness

Begin your meditation sitting up nice and tall in Easy Seat with your hands resting gently, palms upturned, or placed over your heart center. You're ready to bathe everything that surrounds you in light.

1. Focus your attention on your breath as it is in this moment. Follow your natural inhales and exhales

as they enter into your nostrils, travel through your body, settle in your seat, and exit past your lips. If your hands are placed over your chest, feel your chest rise and fall with your breath. Close your eyes for ten full, natural breath cycles. Then open your eyes to read your mantra.

Put Your Heart Chakra to Work . . .

2. Picture your Heart Chakra glowing bright green. Imagine it glowing brighter every time you repeat your mantra. Close your eyes, and on the exhale of each of five breath cycles, repeat either silently or aloud, "I don't seek the light. I am the light." Open your eyes when you're finished.

    Consider those words for just a few moments. You don't have to seek the light. Happiness doesn't live outside of you. You *are* the light. Happiness is what you are in your natural state.

3. Focus on your Heart Chakra once again . . . still glowing bright green, still expanding and contracting with every inhale and exhale. Pure love and happiness radiates from your heart center. It's time to release it into the world. Send this love and happiness out from your heart center. Every time you exhale, the love and happiness is sent farther and farther— first to the immediate area surrounding your physical body, then to the room, then to the space outside of the room. By your last exhale, you're sending pure love and happiness to the entire world.

4. Close your eyes for seven full breath cycles. On each exhale, release more love and happiness into your space. Your Heart Chakra expands with every inhale,

and your exhale releases the light of your Heart Chakra into the world.

Sealing Your Practice . . .

5. Just like your meditation practice is a lighthouse that guides you to your truth, you are a lighthouse that draws others toward the light. Repeat your sealing mantra either silently or aloud on each exhale until you feel ready to reenter your day. "I am light. I am vibrant energy. I am a magnet for the same."

Chapter 7

4 Minutes to Manifest Courage, Confidence, and Success

There were no examples of courage or confidence or success in my immediate family—no one for me to look up to when I was a young person. No one who was financially successful. No one with high self-esteem. It was easy to be fearful because everyone closest to me was afraid.

When I was a kid, the adults in my life said, "Success is really hard." They not only felt it was difficult to achieve, the implication was that it was for other people . . . and not for us. On the one hand, they told me that I was a child of God destined to do great things. On the other hand, they were modeling that we weren't deserving of success and that it wasn't within our reach. I could expect happiness in Heaven, but I shouldn't get my hopes up about dreams coming true in this life. Needless to say, I was confused by these mixed messages and grew up without confidence in my ability to create the life I wanted.

When I began to work on my practice of *guiding* meditation, a lot of those old fears reared their ugly heads. Who was I to try to teach people anything? Who was I to try to write a book? Then I discovered that the courage and confidence I needed for success were intrinsically connected to my sense of purpose. When I remember one of my most important lessons/mantras—"I was created with divine intention"—I again connect to the knowledge that I have a purpose to fulfill. More than anything else, that's what has helped me move forward in spite of fear.

Connecting with your purpose will help you have the courage to act even when fear threatens to hold you back. You'll feel confident that you're *meant* to do something, and that will give you the passion to do it. But how do you know what your purpose is?

Well, I do believe that we each have a unique purpose that is all his/her own. But discovering what that is may not be instantaneous. It can take time to unearth that divine purpose from within you. In the meantime, though, you can still operate in your life with a sense of purpose. I believe there's a common purpose that we all share—to love and to be loved, to learn, and to teach. We're all here to do each of those things in whatever individual way we choose.

For me the love part of that equation is very practical and tangible. It's the love I express on a daily basis toward myself and others. It's earthly love, not just spiritual love. Yes, it's great to be connected to the love of the Universe, but what about your love for the day-to-day moments of your life, the people around you, and the things you're able to do? When I feel that kind of love, I'm invested in this earthly life and my purpose in it. I'm excited about the happiness that can be found in every moment, as we talked about in Chapter 6. I'm excited about what I can do in the world to make it a better place. When I feel and express love, I also feel and express compassion and empathy, both of which connect me to others.

As for *being* loved, it's about allowing myself to receive love from others. This means that while I don't *need* compliments to feel worthy, I do welcome compliments and appreciation from friends, family, colleagues, and students. It means that I allow myself to feel deserving of the love others give me. I acknowledge what I do for other people, and I allow them to praise me or express their gratitude.

This is a key component to discovering how to turn your purpose into a practical way of expressing who you are, and possibly even supporting yourself with a related job. If others appreciate something you do for them, maybe there's a career there.

The next aspect of our common purpose is *to learn*. If you approach life with an open mind and heart, you'll see teachers everywhere—even in the Internet trolls and the haters. Even in the people who treat you poorly. It's the ability to observe your life from a place of curiosity. "I really hate what that person did, and it makes me feel angry. But let me look at that situation. What can I learn from it? How can I prevent something like that from happening again? Is there something inside me that I can change so that I don't attract a similar situation in the future?" Learning is also an expression of love—love of adventure, new experiences, and unique opportunities to discover and grow.

Then, when you've learned a certain amount, it's time to teach others. This can be the scariest part. At least it was for me. You do have to put yourself on the line when you move into the teaching position, but the rewards are enormous. You simply take what you've learned—even if it feels insignificant to you—and share it with others. You can begin by simply sharing the joy of your learning on social media. Tell your story to friends. See if people identify and can use the lessons you've learned in their own lives. Here's an opportunity to share some joy on social media right now.

Spread the Love

My purpose is to love and to be loved,
to learn and to teach. #YH4M

I started by studying yoga and finding a great deal of joy in it. When I became advanced in that practice, I began to teach yoga to others. You don't have to be an absolute expert to be a teacher. You don't have to know all the answers. Remember that perfection doesn't exist. You just need to find the people who know just a little bit less than you at this point, and you pay it forward.

I'm still very humbled in the presence of master yoga teachers. The fear that I'm not worthy comes up for me, but because I have this practice of honoring my purpose, I can ease the fear. There's a great quote by poet Henry Van Dyke: "The woods would be very silent if no birds sang there except those that sang best." If everyone made the demand that they had to be perfect and know everything before they could teach, there would be no teachers.

So much of the time, we tell ourselves that we aren't ready. We believe that we have to learn more, do more, and get more before we can go for the life we want. We think we aren't enough. We say, "If I just lose ten more pounds, I'll be able to have the relationship I want." "If I just get one more degree, I'll be able to have that career I've always dreamed about." Just like we can't wait for peace or happiness to show up, we also can't wait until we're perfect to get on with the business of our purpose. Sure, it makes sense to get some training. I didn't teach a yoga class without ever having studied yoga. But I also didn't wait until I was the master of masters before I started teaching people who could learn from me. We forget that so-called masters aren't perfect either. They're also human. We fail to realize that these people have flaws and fears of their own. We put them on pedestals, but they probably have someone they look up to as well.

I constantly remind myself how ready I am in every single moment. If I waited until I was anxiety-free before I shared my story with the world, you wouldn't be reading this book right now. I would still be working at one of my old jobs (that I hated), wishing I was "ready" to start doing what I'm doing right now. I would never have helped the people I've helped or had all the wonderful rewards I've enjoyed.

There's always someone who can learn from you. Even if you're in the middle of a difficult time in your life, you're right on time. There's enormous reward in teaching. When you make it part of your practice—no matter how small—you'll build tremendous courage and confidence. It will inspire you to learn even more so that you can then pass it on. It's a domino effect that really does gradually change the world for the better.

"A master is a beginner who kept beginning." —Mastin Kipp

Your Unique Purpose

Now that we've talked about our collective purpose—loving, being loved, learning, and teaching—what about your individual purpose that goes beyond the collective? To get clarity about my own, I asked myself three questions while in meditation. Then I listened for whatever answers came to mind, careful not to judge those answers, whatever they were.

1. Who was I before the world told me who to be—
   before society imprinted on my natural way of being?
   I found that I had to ask myself this question
   many times, and the answer changed each time.
   When my students ask themselves this question,
   a common first answer is, "I was a kid who liked
   to color." The next time the question is posed, the
   answer usually goes a bit deeper: "I was someone
   who loved to express myself through coloring and
   was uninhibited in that expression." Eventually
   the answer might be something like "I was fearless,
   confident, insightful, creative, and curious. I knew all
   the answers to the questions of the Universe. I was
   limitless and free." Whoa, that's a big statement! But
   it's also a wonderful truth that can be revealed only
   through a regular practice of exploring, digging, and
   uncovering.

That brings us to Question #2.

2. How would I act, think, move, and express myself if the world had never told me how I had to act? Once you have an answer to this question, you could ask more questions about it: If I were this person who could express without limit, what would I look like? How would I dress? What would I think of myself?

    I've been told so many times in my life by well-meaning people that I should be quieter, and every time it was said, my self-esteem diminished. I felt self-conscious, as if I was doing wrong when I expressed myself freely. So who would I be if no one had ever said that to me?

    And finally we arrive at Question #3.

3. Now that I know who I truly am and how I would express myself if I felt totally free, what am I going to do with that information going forward? This is where the real work of building authentic courage and confidence begins. This is where you start practicing what you know instead of an untruth that you were conditioned to believe. And that can be very scary.

Should You Feel the Fear . . . and Do It Anyway?

Yes, I do feel the fear, and do what I want anyway . . . but with a caveat. Sometimes acting in spite of fear is a white-knuckle experience. The fear is big and makes me tense. I have to fight it while it keeps me in a viselike grip, so everything feels forced and painful. Have you ever had a similar experience? You're shaking in your shoes, but you're trudging forward anyway. It feels akin to trying to walk against the force of a hurricane.

It was a conversation with Josh Becker, host of the *I Simply Am* podcast, that changed how I "felt the fear and did it anyway." At the time he was a stranger, but since then he has become a friend. In that initial discussion, he said something to me that was really hard to take, but it gave me great insight. "I'm hearing how you're talking about your goals," he said. "I'm a great admirer of your work, but you appear desperate." Wow. That felt like a punch to the gut! But I took a breath and made the choice not to be defensive.

"How am I desperate?" I asked. "I don't understand. I feel really good about what I'm doing and the message I'm sharing." I genuinely wanted to know the answer.

"It isn't desperation about wanting anything for yourself. It's desperation that you aren't reaching enough people, that if you don't grow your influence fast enough, people won't get what they need in time," he responded. "But it also feels that you're constantly denying that fear and that you're struggling with it instead of just letting it be and bringing it along with you—accepting that the fear is there."

Ah! I got it instantly. What I'd been doing was relating to my fear as a burden. That awareness alone began to lighten the weight of the fear—not because the fear went away. It didn't! It was still very much there, but I started to relate to it in a subtly different way. I didn't have to think of it as something that was holding me back. I could feel the fear and the courage at the same time. They could live together in me as friends in a way, rather than as adversaries.

In many respects, it was that layering effect again. I was afraid of my fear—afraid that it would get in my way. "Feeling the fear and doing it anyway" works best if we make peace with the fact that the fear is there and find ways to use it. I feel afraid every time I have to get up and speak in front of an audience, for example. My heart races, my thoughts are all over the place, and I'm convinced that I'll sound like a babbling idiot. Even with my advanced self-care/self-love meditation practice, I feel all those things. But I don't try to get rid of the fear. I accept it. I tell myself, "Yes, I'm feeling nervous. This is a natural reaction to public speaking. I also know what I'm talking about, and I have something valuable to share." You see, I can feel the fear, but I can also feel the confidence. I can feel both and still deliver a kick-ass talk. The fear might show up, but it doesn't stop me.

You see, fear is usually an illusion that can be manipulated and changed. The truth is steadfast and powerful. Connect with your truth to cultivate courage and confidence.

When I explain fear to kids, I tell them that I picture it as a big, dark ball of mystery. Then if I ask myself questions about the fear and get curious about it, the mystery becomes smaller and smaller. Even if I don't have answers to all the questions, the curiosity alone begins to "shrink" the ball. I might ask myself, "Where is this fear coming from—a past experience? What's the worst-case scenario, my biggest fear? What's the likelihood that my worst fear could come true? If I let the fear stop me, what are the consequences? For example, what if I never start my teaching work? What if I never write my book?"

In my answers, I weigh the pros and cons, and as I do, the mystery starts to disappear. Let's say the fear is indeed about writing my book. I might answer those questions by saying, "The fear is probably coming from past experiences when I felt ridiculed or like I didn't do something perfectly. The biggest fear is that I'll fall on my face and that everybody will think the book is terrible. But what's the likelihood that my book will be awful? If a publisher decides it's good enough, it must be good enough. Everybody who reads it probably isn't going to like it, but that's OK. I'm sure a lot of people *will* like it. What if I let my fear stop me and I *don't* write my book? What would be the consequences of that? First of all, I'd be disappointed in myself that I gave in to the fear. I'd miss out on the opportunity to grow and help others. I'd miss out on the chance to be the person I want to be." Those are some hefty consequences—worse, in my mind, than the chance of failure. Just clarifying that made me want to do it even more. How could I let my fears stop me from expressing what I know in my heart and soul is my purpose in this life?

Fear doesn't like to be questioned. Nothing that lives in the dark likes to be placed in the spotlight. When we shine light on our fear by questioning it, it starts to cower and diminish. Soon your ball of fear becomes so tiny that it's pocket-size. Then it's merely a tiny, insignificant trifle that you carry around with you, hardly noticing its presence at all—not a giant hurricane that you have to push against or a big, black ball of mystery that weighs you down.

Spread the Love

My fear shrinks when I examine it
with curiosity rather than judgment. #YH4M

As your fear shrinks to a tiny, dark marble of mystery in your pocket, room is made for your divine purpose—the essence of who you were when you arrived in this body—to fill you with passion and joy. You can more easily connect with the courage, confidence, and freedom that you had before you began to feel afraid of being who you are.

CAN FEAR AND LOVE CO-EXIST?

You might have heard that love is the absence of fear or that if we're feeling fear, we're not in a place of love. I don't believe this is true. Fear isn't necessarily the enemy of love. We're human beings, after all, and fear is something we all experience. We aren't so perfect that love happens only in the absence of fear. How unfair would it be if we could love ourselves only if we never felt afraid (which is impossible, by the way)? We can feel fear and still act out of love.

I strongly believe that fear and love can hang out together and be buddies. Both can help us grow and become the teachers we need to lead us to success. Fear can be a motivator as much as it can be a motivation killer. So feel the fear, but act out of love—that's the practice.

Meditating on Fear

When I find myself feeling fear, I don't use a mantra like "I'm brave." I don't pretend that I don't feel fear. To me, bravery isn't about blind faith. It's about acknowledging that fear is present as I'm moving forward. I might even say, "In this moment I'm struggling with fear." When I do that, I allow for possibility. That opening gives me the opportunity to step into success. I'm careful not to say, "I'm afraid." Instead I acknowledge, "I *have* fear."

Remember: you are *not* your fear, but you might *have* some fear right now. *Having* it means it's something you can let go of—like a physical possession that you decide to throw away (or at least not hold on to so tightly). Your fear isn't part of you; it's something *outside* of you. It's a marble in your pocket that you just might be able to throw away someday. That subtle reframe can help the fear begin to dissipate.

Simply acknowledging that I'm struggling with fear in the moment provides me with the possibility for success. My fear might tell me, "You can't," but the truth is that I'm just temporarily struggling with the fear that I can't. I might not believe in myself yet, but I will eventually if I continue to connect with my purpose.

I still carry around pocketfuls of fear marbles, but they don't weigh me down as heavily as they did in the past. Fear still comes up about expressing myself. I'm human, so it's probably inevitable. But I have a strong desire to act on my purpose. I want to speak my truth and let my voice be heard. I don't want to hide or feel that I have to keep my true feelings inside to protect myself or anyone else.

Spread the Love

Speaking my truth is an ultimate expression
of love for others and myself. #YH4M

What have you longed to do but stopped because of fear? What have you worried that you aren't quite ready to do? What does your sense of purpose ask of you? As you meditate, think of what actions you would like to take. If you cultivate the courage and confidence in meditation, what will you do? What will you express?

Meditation for Embracing Fear

Preparation / About This Meditation

I'm finally and gratefully at a place in my life when I can say that fear and I are actually cool with each other. A lot of my precious time has been spent avoiding fear, fighting fear, and too often surrendering to fear. I can't say I don't wish I could get back at least some of that time. I could've been having a lot more fun just doing the things that scared me instead of not doing them at all and feeling regret over it. I did let fear hold me back, and that is a shame. Now I take fear along for the ride, and we're having a pretty awesome time together.

This meditation is called Meditation for Embracing Fear, but that title is probably a bit misleading. This is really a meditation for embracing the fact that fear exists, and that's OK because fear is just an imaginary thing that isn't who you are and can't really stop you from doing anything unless you let it. But that was way too long a name for a meditation!

Fear happens. We can spend a lot of time dissecting it, studying it, or questioning why it's even here in the first place, or we can save all that for a rainy day and get on with the business of allowing it. I'm betting that if you're reading this meditation, fear has been holding you back in some area of your life, and you're ready to move on. Let's not waste another second.

When? Like an unwelcome houseguest, fear has a tendency to pop up unannounced and at the worst possible times. It's like fear can smell when a monumentally important event in your life is about to happen, and it reserves a spot right in the front row. Dead center. And then heckles you from its seat. It plants wildly improbable scenarios in your head—total humiliation, epic failure, or even death! This describes a classic case of stage fright, for instance. In this case, fear looks like a jerk, and you don't have to embrace it if you don't feel like it. But you have to accept it as having a valuable purpose because, otherwise, you risk losing your cool and making *yourself* look like the jerk. So practice this meditation before any event that you anticipate an unannounced pop-in from fear.

There are also circumstances when you may find yourself struggling with an issue or project over a long period of time— plagued by procrastination—and you can't move forward. In this case, fear is in disguise. When its true identity is finally revealed, fear can teach you how to recognize and remove blocks. But you don't have to spend a lot of time uncovering your fear or what it's trying to teach you. Just acknowledging that there's something to be learned can reveal the lesson. Practice this meditation in times of prolonged struggle or procrastination to give fear space to reveal its true self.

Where? Practice embracing your fear in your favorite meditation space or wherever you happen to be when you most need this meditation.

Position? Sit in your relaxed Easy Seat with your hands resting on your thighs or knees, and your palms upturned. A relaxed seat still requires you to sit up nice and tall. Energy should be allowed to flow freely through your body from your crown to your seat. Just make sure you're not too stiff—tensing your muscles can interrupt that flow.

Open and close your eyes when guided.

You Have 4 Minutes to Become Friends with Fear

Fear has been a part of your life for a long time now, and sometimes it's held you back from experiencing all the good that life has in store for you. Let's transform fear from a burden that weighs you down into your new traveling companion. Fear is coming along for the ride, but you're in control of the route.

1. Focus your attention on your breath as it is in this moment. Carefully examine the characteristics of your natural inhales and exhales. Are they fast or slow, shallow or deep? Continue to follow your breath without trying to change it in any way.

2. Scan your body from the crown of your head down toward your seat, and then through your legs to the tips of your toes. As you scan each part of your body, release any muscle tension that you may be holding. Do this by inhaling fully and releasing the muscle tension with big, letting-go exhales. Allow yourself enough time—up to ten breath cycles—to scan your body thoroughly.

3. Allow your focus to return to your breath. Begin practicing Even Breath, matching the duration of each exhale to the duration of the inhale before it.

    You are in control of your thoughts, your breath, and your actions. Fear has no power over you. You are about to send a very clear message to the Universe that you are not led by fear. You are the navigator on this journey.

4. Read your first mantra, and then close your eyes (or soften the focus of your vision) to repeat it on the exhale of five full breath cycles. Repeat your mantras out loud if that feels comfortable. After you're finished with the first mantra, move on to the second.

Mantra 1

I have fear, but I'm not afraid.

Mantra 2

Fear is a teacher bearing gifts. I'm open to the lessons.

5. Return to your Even Breath, placing all attention on maintaining its steady pace. You feel safe, relaxed, and at peace. You are assured in your ability to keep calm and face your fear.

6. Continue with your Even Breath for as long as it feels good. When you're ready, open your eyes and return to your day.

Meditation for Confidence

Preparation / About This Meditation

Once you truly accept that you are divine love totally connected to your purpose, expressing yourself freely is so much easier. Doubt feeds fear; knowing inspires confidence.

Confidence is the wonderful by-product of the realization of your purpose, combined with the dutiful dedication to expressing that purpose. You've been given a very important mission that you must fulfill, and carrying out that mission is going to require a bit of confidence. Be warned—sharing your purpose with others might not feel so great sometimes. It could be downright terrifying.

Confidence doesn't manifest only in the absence of fear. You can feel fear and still express yourself confidently. Because you're supported by the divine power that set you on your mission in the first place, you can have fear and still play the part of an influential spreader of light. The Universe wants you to share your purpose;

it wants you to succeed. Stifling your voice denies the whole world of divine love and healing truth.

Dr. Maya Angelou famously said, "When you get, give. When you learn, teach." You've been blessed with purpose and a voice to express it. You have a big job to do, so let's set you up with a meditation to support your good work.

When? Practice your confidence meditation when you're having trouble expressing yourself freely. You could start your day with this meditation or use it in times when you need a little extra support standing up for yourself—an important business meeting, a holiday dinner with family, or a heavy discussion with a loved one or significant other.

Where? If you've gone through the chapters one by one, you're halfway through the 27 meditations in this book, and I hope you've been able to secure a favorite meditation spot for yourself by now. It's important that you not only make time in your day for meditation but that you also create physical space for your practice. Your space can be a dedicated room, a pantry, or the front seat of your car. My laundry room is still my go-to spot. It's important only that your space allows you to feel safe and that you can meditate without interruption.

Position? Sit up tall in Easy Seat. You should not only feel strong in your seat, but you should appear strong, too. Refer back to the pose cues for Easy Seat in Chapter 2 if you need help getting into the position comfortably while observing proper alignment.

Rest your hands on your thighs or knees in Kubera Mudra by placing the tips of your bent ring and pinkie fingers on the middle of each palm and connecting the tips of the remaining three fingers. This mudra is indicated for confidence, and it will help imprint your mantras into your subconscious.

Keep your eyes open to read each step of your meditation and closed, if you can, while reciting your mantras.

You Have 4 Minutes to Express Yourself with Courage

The Universe has gifted you with purpose and perspective and also with a unique voice to express each to the world. It's your mission to honor your voice by sharing it freely—for your own happiness and the happiness of those who surround you. Be confident in knowing that sharing your voice is an expression of gratitude to the Universe and an extension of God's love for the world.

1. Sitting in Easy Seat with your eyes closed (or the focus of your vision softened) and your hands in Kubera Mudra, begin to breathe deeply, filling your entire body all the way down to your seat with every inhale, and allowing your exhales to empty every bit of breath from your body. Pause at the bottom of each exhale before inhaling again. Practice this pattern of breathing for at least ten full breath cycles. Then open your eyes to read your mantras.

    You're already feeling heightened levels of energy in your entire body. A tingling vibration runs up and down your arms and legs—you feel it in your fingers and toes. With each inhale, you draw more life force into your body. You're drawing on the power of the Universe to energetically nurture the seeds of courage that have already been planted inside of you. Your physical body is prepared to receive the full intention of your mantras.

2. Read your first mantra. Then close your eyes and repeat it either silently or aloud on each exhale of five breath cycles. When you're finished, read your next mantra, and then repeat it for another five breath cycles.

Mantra 1

I honor my purpose by speaking my truth.

Mantra 2

Speaking my truth is an expression
of love for others and myself.

3. Continue with your big inhales and exhales. Energy
    is flowing freely in and around you. Notice how
    you're sitting up taller, how your chest is wide
    open to the front of you, and how your whole body
    appears to be more awake.

4. Seal your practice by repeating one last mantra on
    each exhale for three breath cycles: "I love who I am.
    I love what I have to say."

Meditation for Taking Action

Preparation / About This Meditation

You haven't eliminated fear, but you've accepted it as just
another part of life. You've been blessed with ideas and desires
and a unique voice, which are begging to be set free, and you
understand now that it's your duty to share these divine truths;
the Universe commands it! You're ready for the next step—the
part of the journey where you make the transition from focusing
your attention inward to sending your loving energy outward.

Success, happiness, and becoming an influential teacher to
others are all part of your inevitable fate. You've been given the
tools, so you have no choice but to move toward success with confident enthusiasm. To choose otherwise denies truths and wastes
precious time. You're ready, and the world is waiting for you.

Let's get down to the business of spreading some love. This is
the fun part! You get to gather up all that you've learned in the first
seven chapters of this book and put it to work—not just for you but
for other people, too. It's important to understand that even small
efforts can lead to a huge outcome. You can shift consciousness
and change the physical world by sharing your purpose, no matter

how grand or simple. It really is true that when you've touched just one person's heart, you've changed the whole world forever.

The work isn't difficult. It's just a matter of taking one step at a time, despite the presence of fear. You're empowered by the support of your loving creator and your duty to fulfill your purpose. Love, be loved, learn, and teach. Consistently show up, and always move onward. Know that the Universe has your back. Allow yourself to have fear, but know that it can't stop you. Stick it in your pocket and carry on.

When? When the Universe calls on you to take action, show up prepared! Practice this meditation regularly to nurture a disciplined forward movement toward your goals. Weekday mornings before work are a great time to practice your Meditation for Taking Action.

Call on the power of this meditation whenever energetic paralysis sets in. If you're stuck in a rut of procrastination, let this meditation guide your first step out of it.

Where? Practice in any quiet space where you feel comfortable. This is a powerful meditation meant to inspire action. Reading your mantras out loud in a private meditation space may make the meditation even more potent.

Position? Sit up tall in your Easy Seat. Once again, I'm going to guide you to use the Kubera Mudra. If you prefer not to use hand mudras, place your hands with palms upturned on your thighs or knees.

Can you concentrate on your meditation with your eyes open? Let's find out! After reading each instruction, keep your eyes open and focus your vision on a single object.

You Have 4 Minutes to Feel the Fear and Do It Anyway

You have fear, but you're not afraid. You have the tools. You possess the knowledge. The Universe has your back. You're ready to take the next step toward your inevitable success. Let's get started.

1. Sitting in your Easy Seat with your hands in Kubera Mudra (if you choose), focus your attention on your natural breath. If you're feeling any anxiety, allow each breath to affirm that you're safe in this moment. Silently count each breath cycle of one full inhale and exhale all the way to 10.

   1 ... 2 ... 3 ... 4 ... 5 ... 6 ... 7 ... 8 ... 9 ... 10

   Notice how your breath has already changed to become quieter and calmer. Notice how your body is more relaxed. You're ready to set your journey to success in motion.

2. With your eyes open and your vision focused softly on an object in front of you, repeat each of your mantras out loud on the exhale for five full breath cycles.

Mantra 1

The Universe supports me. Success is waiting for me.

Mantra 2

I am not physically stuck. I move easily through fear.

   Fear can only keep you stuck if you choose to be stuck. It's your choice to take action in every moment. Fear is along for the ride; you're the captain of your vessel.

3. Read the following words out loud, taking your time
    to fully absorb the spirit of the message. When you're
    finished, take one last big breath and return to your
    day. "Today I will put myself out there—unafraid and
    knowing that I already have everything I need to be
    successful. I will not say, 'I can't do this.' Instead I
    will say, 'At this moment, I'm struggling with this.'
    When I create possibility and room for success,
    I step easily into the role of a successful person.
    My mistakes, my faults, and my less-than-perfect
    decisions have all been in service to my journey
    toward enlightened success. I have nothing to fear. I
    am supported in my efforts."

Chapter 8

4 Minutes to Heal Your Relationship or Attract the One You Want

When I was a toddler, my family stopped celebrating Christmas. My parents said it was because of religion, financial issues, and antimaterialism beliefs. Once I started school, I felt a lot of shame about it. I had to try to explain to my friends why we were Christian but didn't acknowledge Christmas.

One day I overheard my mother say, "If a man ever came into my life, and it was really important to him, I'd celebrate Christmas again." I instantly understood that it didn't matter to her that Christmas was important to her children. She would change only if it were important to a man. She even said, "Your husband is the most important person in your life. Everyone else comes after him." My mother wasn't making the argument that a strong relationship with her partner was the foundation for a happy family—I believe that to be true and practice that belief in my own life. She was saying that the men in her life mattered more than us.

When I was 10 years old and my younger sister was 7 (after our parents had split up), my mother entered into a relationship with someone we called our stepfather, even though he and my mother never got married. True to her word, my mother let us observe Christmas again because it was what the new man in her life wanted. She demonstrated what I already feared to be true.

This was only one of many relationships when my mother placed the needs and desires of the men in her life above those of her children and even herself. I watched her devalue herself for their affection over and over. And I internalized it. Through my mother's actions and words, I was taught that women simply weren't as important as men. As a result, I grew up not only devaluing myself as a girl, but also not valuing girls as friends.

I was always that girl who was a bit of a tomboy and had better relationships with boys. In high school my boyfriend was my best friend, and my friendships with other girls were superficial. When I did have one good girlfriend, she would always get pushed aside for the boy.

In my mind, girls would come and go, but a boy was somebody you wanted to stay. He had value and was held in high regard. Because of what I'd been taught, I simply didn't see women as valuable in my life. I didn't see why I needed them. I believed that girls were competitive, catty, and backstabbing, so I was afraid to let them get too close to me. But the truth was that I was the one who was judgmental and disloyal. I can recall, even as early as age 10, feeling jealous of other girls at school who had pretty clothes, and I felt unworthy of approaching them for friendship. So I attracted girls who were a perfect reflection of me rather than the kinds of girls who could be true friends. After all, I wasn't yet capable of being a true friend to them.

I wasn't a true friend to myself either. When you view women as having no value, you have to include yourself in that club. As I continued the pattern of holding men in such high regard that I stayed with them regardless of their faults, I also accepted a lot of abuse that I should never have accepted.

Like most girls, I modeled myself after my mother, and she had never healed her own relationship with herself or with her own mother. So there it was—that constant yearning to be made whole by a relationship with a man.

Learning to Be Alone

When I first entered into romantic relationships, it was painful for me to spend time alone. If the man in my life had to go out of town for some reason, it was awful because I had no one else to be with. I had made him so central that I had alienated myself from other relationships—particularly friendships with women. My self-love was so dependent upon the constant attention of a man that when he was missing, there was nothing else there—nothing but me feeling needy.

As I look back on that time in my life, I realize that it must have been terrible to be in a relationship with me. I made the man feel guilty if he didn't give me the attention I craved 24/7.

When my first marriage crumbled, I was terrified because, even though it was a toxic relationship, I had relied on him for so much. And I played that game with myself that so many of us play when we suffer a breakup: "If I had been prettier, he would have stayed . . ." "If I had been sweeter, he would have stayed . . ." If, if, if . . ."If I had been enough, he would have stayed . . ."

Today my life is completely different. When my husband travels, I miss him, but it's also a nice period of time for me to be by myself. Now when I'm alone, I like who I am, and I enjoy my own company. But it took some work for me to get to that place, and meditation helped me immensely.

Part of the practice for me—which wasn't always easy—became "Who am I without this person?" I started by taking inventory of what I valued about myself. At first I had to borrow what other people had said about me because I didn't yet trust that I had good qualities. I know teachers always say that you have to find your self-esteem from within—I've said it already in this book—but writing down the good things that others said about me helped me begin to believe that they were right. So, yes, it's true that relying on others to provide us with our sense of self-worth keeps us on unsteady ground, but compliments from people who care about us can indeed help. It's natural to enjoy receiving praise from others. A problem arises only when we're a vacuum inside with no self-worth generated from within.

Spread the Love

I value the good people in my life, and their good opinions of me are something I value, too. #YH4M

So my way of developing that self-love from the inside out was by taking what I was given from the outside in. I started to keep a list of the compliments I received. Someone once said something nice about my eyelashes. I wrote it down.

My belief in my inventory was tentative at first. I was a bit like that old *Saturday Night Live* character Stuart Smalley, who would look in the mirror and say his affirmations without really believing them. I wrote, "I'm smart, I'm ambitious, I know how to organize really well." Then I wrote, "Somebody out there will think I'm pretty." That was the best I could do at the time. To keep a sense of humor about it, I actually called it my "Pathetic Affirmation Journal."

I had my first child when I was 18, so by the time I divorced at 28, I already had three kids. I felt unattractive and was horrified at the thought of anyone seeing me naked. I felt unacceptable.

Slowly but surely, though, I began to absorb my inventory and realize that what I was writing was true. I really was smart. I really was pretty. I really was ambitious and talented.

Carrying Baggage into Relationships

During this time that I was struggling to lift my self-esteem and recover from my divorce, lo and behold, a new man came into my life—the man who would eventually become my forever husband. In the beginning I was in fake-it-till-you-make-it mode. I dressed up and tried to be the woman I wanted to be—the woman I thought he deserved, even if I didn't feel like I really was.

I was so insecure, though, that I broke up with him almost once a month. I concocted all sorts of excuses as to why our relationship would never work. I even broke up with him because he didn't get up early enough in the morning. "I have children, so it isn't OK that you don't wake up until two o'clock in the afternoon," I told him. I realize now that I did this only because I didn't feel deserving of him. But it's also true that we weren't a match on an energetic level—not yet. He was in a better place emotionally than I was. I needed to become more independent. I needed to get to that place where I could watch him go on a trip and still enjoy my time alone. I had to truly understand my value in order to be his energetic equal. I didn't have to be perfect for us to work, but as my sense of self-worth improved, our relationship improved exponentially along with it.

I'm so lucky that in spite of my behavior, he remained convinced that we were right for each other. He saw the potential in me, and he was persistent—even though he has since admitted that our first years together were rough for him. Nevertheless, he wouldn't let me push him away, and I am eternally grateful for his fortitude.

There's no way to avoid carrying baggage into relationships, but the more I used meditation and mantras, as well as books and seminars, to begin to let go of some of that baggage, the better our relationship became. I also became a better friend to the women in my life and a better friend to myself.

Icing on the Cake

As my self-worth increased, I began to enjoy my alone time, and I no longer needed my husband to fill that vacuum inside me. When my self-worth was dependent on others, especially my husband, it was always in a fragile state. After all, even in the happiest of relationships, there's an ebb and flow of affection. You'll always be left yearning because the moment your spouse has an off day, you'll feel abandoned.

I also began to value myself as a woman, and that translated into valuing women more as a gender. As I became a better friend to myself, I opened up to being able to be a good friend to other women.

Suddenly, for the first time, I started to attract amazing friendships. Out of the blue, a woman would ask me if she could help me in some way. I'll admit that I approached it with a bit of skepticism. It was so new to me. "Is she for real? What does she want from me?"

The first time it happened, it was a woman I ran into on the street. "Our kids play soccer together," she said. Even though I had just had my fourth baby, I had never really had close relationships with other moms—well, not with regular moms. (I did have my small crew of punk-rock moms from Staten Island who had had babies at the same time I had, but I'd lost touch with them when I'd moved back to New Jersey before my third baby was born.)

The other soccer mom started talking to me, and she offered to walk with me every day so that we could both get in shape. Our walks turned out to be a lot of fun, and we fell into an easy friendship. As we shared more personal information about ourselves, I disclosed some feelings I'd been having after the birth of my child. She recognized that I had postpartum depression and gave me strict instructions: "Tell your husband you've been struggling and that you're scared. So the next time you go to the midwife together, you can still tell her you're 'fine,' and *he'll* tell her the truth." By doing this, she saved me, and I got the help I needed. We're still friends today.

Then women started to help me in my professional life, and I developed a number of very close and beautiful friendships with those women. They continue to support me, and I support them in turn. I have even attracted a mentor—an older woman who has become like a second mother to me. Actually she has been a mother to me in a way that my biological mother was never capable of being, due to her own pain and baggage.

Now, even though I have a great marriage, I feel that my life wouldn't be complete without these relationships with women. I have finally discovered what the sisterhood is all about!

Spread the Love

I have to be a true friend to have true friends. I attract who I am. #YH4M

These women showed up in my life because I was able to use meditation and mantras to slowly love and value myself more. That doesn't mean I'm walking around loving myself perfectly every day. Loving ourselves is not a narcissistic adventure. I don't look in the mirror every morning and say, "I'm the most beautiful woman on the planet! I'm the smartest! I'm the greatest!" Like I said in the body chapter, I don't have to adore everything about my body or think I'm the greatest thing since mint chocolate-chip ice cream. What I've evolved into is someone who looks in the mirror and says, "This is what I'm working with. This is cool. I like it, and I think the right people will like it, too. I'm cool with being me, and I wouldn't trade places with anyone else. I feel comfortable in my own skin. I'm a complete, whole, and worthy person who's deserving of love." And as a result, I attract people who reflect that belief. Haters don't dare enter my space because they can feel that I'm not going to pay them any mind.

I have learned that when we enter a relationship with a deficit—as I did in my first marriage and in the beginning of my current marriage—we're starving, and the relationship is just a

Band-Aid on an open wound. When we're starving, we'll take any-thing—fast food that isn't nutritious . . . and abusive relationships with mean girls and dangerous men.

When, on the other hand, we enter a relationship full with our own sense of self-worth, we have the patience to wait for a good, nourishing meal that we can savor and enjoy. We don't *need* it to fill an empty life. We simply *want* it to make life even better. And the good life that we create when we're alone doesn't come from wealth or beauty or professional success. It comes from self-worth.

The more I learned to accept and appreciate myself, the more the love I received from others was icing on the cake. And the more I believed I was worthy of love, the more love came my way.

Meditation for Self-Reflection

Preparation / About This Meditation

To find peace in a chaotic environment, I practice *allowing*. I allow what is, release worry about what I can't control, and focus my attention only on things I can actually change—my thoughts, my words, and my actions.

To find resolution in conflicts with other people, I practice *awareness*. I challenge myself to answer questions that reveal how I'm showing up for the relationship. I ask myself, "What part am I playing in this struggle?" and "Am I communicating with love or with judgment?"

In your Meditation for Happiness, I guided you to recite, "I am light. I am vibrant energy. I am a magnet for the same." Being a *magnet for the same* is great if what you are is light and vibrant energy. But what happens if you're angry, insecure, or just generally unhappy? The same rule applies—you're a magnet for the same.

In this meditation for self-reflection, you're going to practice sending love and light to all the places that need it most. But first you have to identify those places. I'm going to guide you to ask a question inspired by my friend Meggan Watterson, a celebrated author and spiritual teacher: "Where has my love not yet reached?"

Asking questions during meditation can be as beneficial as reciting positive mantras. When you ask yourself the right questions, answers are revealed without much effort. Once the answers become known, you can begin the process of healing and growth.

Then your *showing up for love* mantras will remind you of how powerful you are when it comes to attracting everything you desire. Use these mantras as regular reminders to keep negativity in check and to connect to your true nature of love and divine intention.

When? Holding up a mirror to your true self is no minor task. This meditation can bring up some realizations that you need to process. Whatever time of day you choose for your meditation, make sure you have at least a little while to regroup before returning to your regular activities. You may discover that waiting until your day is done is best for practicing potentially intense meditations.

Where? For the same reason that you might need extra time for your meditation, make sure that you feel safe and secure in your meditation space. This one is best practiced in a comfortable, familiar, and private place.

Position? A relaxed Easy Seat and Semireclined Bound Angle Pose are two perfect poses for supporting safe vulnerability and openness to new information. Choose the one you prefer.

In either pose allow your hands to rest gently with palms upturned.

Close your eyes, if you can, after asking your question and while repeating your mantras.

You Have 4 Minutes to Get Real about How You're Showing Up for Love

"Where has my love not yet reached?" You're going to open your heart to receive the answer to this question during your time in meditation. The Universe and your own inner wisdom will show you exactly how to become a person who easily attracts healthy, fulfilling relationships.

Get settled into your chosen position, and ready yourself for your meditation.

1. Begin your meditation by setting a loving intention. Repeat these words, either silently or aloud: "I've done my best with the tools that were available to me. Sometimes my best served me well, and sometimes my efforts came up short. I hold no judgment toward my former self. I'm showing up now with nothing but pure intention. I want to be the best person I can be, and I welcome all compassionate guidance."

2. Allow yourself to breathe naturally, focusing on your easy inhales and exhales. There's no need to change your breathing in this moment.

3. Bring your attention to your Third Eye Chakra (the space on your forehead between your eyebrows). Wisdom enters your body through this chakra. Imagine this space glowing with a gentle indigo-colored light that expands and contracts with your inhales and exhales.

4. Close your eyes (or soften the focus of your vision) and concentrate on this beautiful indigo light for ten full breath cycles. Reopen your eyes for your next instruction.

   Now it's time to ask yourself "Where has my love not yet reached?" Listen for the answer. Let me take just a moment to explain this a little further. The "where" can be any area where you've placed harsh criticism or judgment instead of love. It can be a time when you've withheld compassion or understanding. Have there been times when you've chosen lashing out over listening? This isn't just about other people. Where has your love not yet reached inside *you*?

5. Close your eyes once again for your question. Concentrating on your Third Eye Chakra and its glowing indigo light, speak your question out loud or silently to yourself. "Where has my love not yet reached?" Take a moment to receive the answer. Just one place will do for now.

6. Once you have your answer, bring your attention to your Heart Chakra, glowing green as it expands and contracts with your inhales and exhales. Just like in your Meditation for Happiness, you're going to send love from your Heart Chakra directly to the place revealed to you in your answer. With your eyes closed, imagine the green light of your Heart Chakra traveling directly to that place and bathing it in its loving glow.

The Healing Has Begun . . .

You have been guided by the Universe toward the part of you that hasn't quite been showing up for love, and the healing is already taking place. You know where love has been missing, and you know exactly how to send it there.

7. Seal your meditation by repeating a mantra of self-assurance. Close your eyes one last time, and recite your mantra on each exhale of five breath cycles. When you're finished, open your eyes and give yourself some time to reflect on your experience before reentering your day. Your mantra is "I attract what I believe about myself. I attract who I am."

Meditation for Attracting True Love

Preparation / About This Meditation

The first time I ever went camping was with my husband. We had been dating less than a year when we planned a weekend of wilderness camping in the New Jersey Pine Barrens. We each lugged 75 pounds of equipment, food, and water on our backs, down sandy trails to our site, and spent the next three days and two nights collecting wood, cooking over our campfire, and falling asleep under the stars to the sounds of whip-poor-wills.

Sounds magical, right?

It was absolutely dreadful.

I relished spending the time alone with my love, but sleeping outside without access to a bathroom or running water was the exact opposite of my idea of a romantic weekend. Camping was *his* thing, not mine. As a dutiful girlfriend trying to win the affections of my new man, I *pretended* to like camping.

He was happy, I was miserable, and my plan was working perfectly . . . until afterward when he started asking to go camping all the time. I realized that the charade I had started was completely unsustainable. I would have to fess up fast or risk a lifetime of summers spent pooping in the woods.

This, of course, is a harmless (except for the bug bites) example of pretending for love. Too often we pretend to be something we're not or do things we don't want to do in an effort to win the love, affection, or admiration of someone we care about. And what does that get us? When we show up for love wearing a disguise, how can we ever know if we're being loved for who we are and not just for what we appear to be? Wouldn't it be better to decide that we are lovable as is—as God loves us—and allow *true* love to bloom?

I did eventually admit my deep disdain for sleeping outside, but we still go camping every once in a great while. What's different now is that my husband knows that I'm doing it because I love him, and I love seeing him enjoy himself. In return, he suffers through movies of Jane Austen novels and the *very* occasional yoga class.

When? Start your day affirming that you're totally and completely worthy of great love, just as you are. Greet the sun with your authentic self, and let the Universe know that you're ready and open to receive love.

Where? Meditate in your quiet morning spot—in bed or any private space in your home. A seat next to a sunny window may help to invite joy into your heart. If weather permits, a meditation outside can be even more uplifting.

Position? Sit in your Easy Seat and place your hands on your thighs or knees with your palms upturned. Radiant energy attracts radiant energy, so make sure your posture is tall, and the line from the crown of your head to the base of your spine is long and straight.

Close your eyes when guided or, as always, maintain a very soft visual focus if you're uncomfortable closing your eyes.

You Have 4 Minutes to Welcome the Love You Deserve

It's a brand-new day, and you're ready to let love in. Start your meditation by focusing your attention on your natural inhales and exhales. Allow each breath to affirm that you are a living, breathing child of God, blessed in this moment.

1. Allow yourself to follow your easy, natural inhales and exhales for ten full breath cycles. Feel the air enter through your nostrils, pass down the back of your throat, fill your lungs and your belly, rest in your seat, and then return to the outside through your mouth. Each breath awakens and energizes you more.

2. Close your eyes and start to imagine a white light glowing brightly above your head. Focus on this light as it expands and contracts with each inhale and exhale for five full breath cycles. Then open your eyes for your next instruction.

3. Take a few moments to allow your glowing white light to fill your entire body and warm you from within. The light will enter your body through the crown of your head and slowly fill your whole body with its gentle, warming energy. This light is God's love. It is pure love, delivered to you as a gift from your benevolent creator. Close your eyes for ten full breath cycles and feel love's light flow through your body.

   You were created from divine love, and divine love blesses you with its light. Your inner light shines brightly and attracts more loving light toward you all the time. There is nothing you need to say or do to make your light shine. You are love and light, just as you are.

4. Close your eyes and read each of the following three mantras either silently or aloud on the exhale of three full breath cycles, stopping to open your eyes after each mantra and read the next. Reciting these mantras will seal your practice and infuse every cell of your body with loving, light-filled energy. When you're finished, open your eyes and continue with the rest of your morning routine. You will draw loving energy toward you throughout your entire day.

Mantra 1

I am a complete person, deserving of love.

Mantra 2

I attract true love when I express myself authentically.

Mantra 3

I have so much good to offer, just as I am.

Meditation for Ultimate and Lasting Love

Preparation / About This Meditation

Love maintains itself. There's no need to tend to it or "keep it alive." You can't kill love. When you're experiencing a lack or loss of love in a relationship, love is simply being edged out by all the stuff that *isn't* love—jealously, selfishness, insecurity, busyness, desperation, and fear—manifestations of ego.

Dr. Wayne W. Dyer used to say that "ego" was an acronym for "edging God out." If ego is the representation of fear, and God is love, then the presence of ego and every emotion that is fear-based literally pushes love out of our lives. Love is ever-present in the Universe, but it's our job to make room for it in our relationships.

This starts with cultivating the knowing that the love part is easy. We don't have to work hard on keeping love around. The work is in keeping fear at bay. Approach love with love, not with fear. Release attachment; invite security. Release desperation; invite abundance. Release the feeling of not being enough; invite the knowing that lasting love happens when two people love themselves completely.

When? Practice this meditation at any time of the day. It's appropriate in times when you're experiencing total fulfillment in your romantic relationship and in times of struggle. Before you begin, it might be helpful to revisit the question from your Meditation for Self-Reflection, but with a small change. Ask yourself, "Where haven't I been sending my love?"

Where? Settle into a safe, comfortable spot, free from distraction.

Position? Practice your meditation in Easy Seat, sitting up tall with the palms of your hands resting gently on your thighs or knees.

Your eyes will be open at the beginning of your practice and closed for the remainder. You'll have only one message to read at the beginning, and the rest of your time will be spent in quiet reflection.

Practice with a Twist: Turn this into a couple's meditation! Let me offer you a twist on this meditation that can be an incredible bonding experience for you and your significant other.

1. Sit back-to-back in Easy Seat with your bodies touching at your shoulders and bottoms.

2. As one of you inhales, the other exhales, and vice versa. Pay close attention to the energy passing between you as you breathe in and out. Feel your partner's back expand and contract with each breath. Practice breathing like this for a minute or so before you begin your meditation.

You Have 4 Minutes to Create a Love That Lasts a Lifetime

Whether you're practicing alone or with your partner, the steps of this meditation are basically the same. This is a simple meditation in which you'll read a message and spend the rest of the time on your seat in quiet and careful contemplation of that message.

1. Read the following words either silently or aloud. If you're practicing with a partner, choose one of you to read it out loud. Take time to read the words slowly. At the end of each sentence, pause for a breath before continuing. "I love myself so fully and so deeply that the love I receive from others is just icing on the cake. I have no need for someone to complete me. There is no lack in my life. There's only the pleasure and excitement of seeing what new experiences, opportunities, and miracles are born out of the love I share with my partner."

2. Close your eyes and allow those words to settle into your physical self. Feel them travel on your breath to every part of your body—through your arms to your fingertips, and your legs to your toes. Feel your body fill up with the meaning of what you just declared.

You love yourself deeply. You need no one to complete you. There is no lack. There is only pleasure. Love expands all good things.

3. Continue with your long inhales and exhales for as long as you'd like. When you're finished, take one last big inhale and audible exhale, and then return to your day. If you're practicing with a partner, give each other a great, big hug.

Chapter 9

4 Minutes to Ease Grief and the Pain of Loss

In April 2013 my father lost a nearly seven-year battle with several different types of cancer. When he reached the age of 70, it was an even bigger milestone than usual because, frankly, no one had expected him to live that long. Those last years of his life, everyone in the family made sure they didn't miss any of our holiday gatherings. We knew all too well that any one of them could be his last.

When he finally left us, there were no feelings of shock. There was no sense of being overwhelmed. We had been gradually letting him go over a long period of time. Everyone felt it was time for him to stop suffering. So, in many ways, it was a relief that he could be released from a body that wasn't able to serve him anymore.

We were all by his bedside when he passed, and I felt honored to be present for what was a peaceful and beautiful transition. In fact, that experience is part of the inspiration for my becoming a birth doula. I watched someone pass out of life, and I wanted to help others bring new life into the world. It's a way I can be part of life's greatest mysteries.

My mother, unlike my father, was vibrant, healthy, and actively involved in life. "She'll outlive us all!" everyone frequently said. But just seven months after my father's death, my mother suffered a massive stroke while on vacation in North Carolina. This time it was so sudden—a complete shock.

Luckily my two sisters and I were able to go to North Carolina and spend time with our mother. That time turned out to be the last 10 days of her life.

Two days after her stroke and our arrival at the hospital, we were told that Mom had a condition called locked-in syndrome. She was physically paralyzed but fully aware of everything going on around her. The only parts of her body that she could control were her eyes.

In a miraculous turn of events, my younger sister had recently watched the movie *The Diving Bell and the Butterfly*, the story of someone with this same syndrome. It was only by random circumstance that she had seen the movie, and it inspired her so much that she ended up doing extensive research on the syndrome. As a result of this (probably divinely coordinated) coincidence, she said, "I already know all about this! Here's what we need."

She led us to the store to buy poster boards and markers, and we set up the exact kinds of charts that help people with locked-in syndrome to communicate. With these tools, my mother was not only able to communicate with us but she also was able to rewrite her will, express her final wishes, and tell us how she felt about us.

Of course, when all you can use to communicate is the blinking of your eyes, there isn't much room for the nuances of conversation. When my mother had her stroke, the two of us hadn't spoken to each other for three months. We had engaged in a lifelong cycle of talking to each other five times a day and then erupting in an argument over some past unresolved issue and not speaking for months—sometimes even years—at a time. The period before her stroke was one of those postargument times.

When I walked into her hospital room, I had no way of knowing if I'd ever be able to speak to her again . . . or even if she'd want me there in the room if/when she woke up. It was scary and emotional.

Once we were told that she wouldn't recover and that she could communicate only by blinking, I knew it was my last opportunity to clear up the issues between us. We couldn't have a normal conversation about what had happened. We couldn't talk it out like we'd been able to do in the past. So I had to make my words precise and pristine. "I love you very much," I told her. "I've missed you, and I'm happy that I can be here for you. I support any decision you make for yourself."

Within a matter of days, Mom made the decision to be taken off of life support. She didn't want to stay trapped in a body that no longer worked. So I said, "I know you're only passing into another stage of life. If you continue to send me messages, I'll look for them and talk to you all the time."

While we couldn't talk about our disagreement in the normal way, that really didn't matter anymore. As her final message, she blinked the following to me and to my sisters: "Miss you three."

It was an enormous gift to be able to communicate with our mother in those last days, but I was still left with a tremendous sense of regret. I couldn't even express my grief. I think I blocked it because it would have meant also connecting with my guilt. I judged myself for missing my mother and wanting her back . . . when I felt I hadn't fully appreciated my relationship with her when she was still with us.

Even if we have a chance to say our piece before someone passes away, there's always plenty unsaid. We never have enough time. We don't just lose seeing the person every day and sharing the news of our lives. We lose the ability to fix the relationship. That power is no longer in our hands. How can we resolve what was unresolved when the person is no longer around? That loss of control adds another layer to the grief.

Obviously my experience of my mother's death was in sharp contrast to what I experienced after my father's. There was no preparation for what happened to Mom. It was out of nowhere. That made my grief over her loss more complicated.

Pain That Changes You

Like most everyone, I've suffered many losses in my life, including my divorce from my first husband. But I've also experienced loss of friendships, jobs, and all sorts of other things. Saying good-bye to some*one* or some*thing* we want to keep is never easy.

One of the turning points for me came when I was in a spin class with *The Biggest Loser* trainer and creator of the "20-Minute Body" workout program, Brett Hoebel. He was yelling out different motivational phrases in class, and one really got to me: "There are two types of pain—pain that hurts you and pain that changes you."

In that moment I realized that my pain had been continuously hurting me. And while it had also been changing me, it was changing me in a negative way. It was making me more afraid, more closed off, and more bitter. I was inspired in that moment to stop looking at pain as something that hurts me. I decided that I could look at my pain instead as a catalyst for change, for making me better, and for preparing me for the inevitable loss and grief that would happen at different points in my life.

It isn't as though my pain was gone in an instant, but thinking of each loss as an opportunity instead of a burden created a huge shift for me. It helped me to see that I could manage my emotional reactions to loss and prevent those feelings from consuming me. Again, the losses can become fertilizer that bears fruit in our lives, but only if we allow the growth to take place.

I believe our feelings wouldn't exist without a higher purpose. It's when we don't attach any positive purpose to our emotions that they become stuck within us. Or when we attach a negative purpose to our feelings—such as believing that we're being punished by God or fate or karma. When we think we deserve our pain or think of ourselves as victims, our emotions tend to fester or spiral out of control.

Spread the Love

I choose to be changed—for the better—by my pain.
I choose to let go and to learn. #YH4M

Attachment and Acceptance

Buddhist and Yogic philosophies teach us that attachment to physical things will cause us pain because those things are impermanent. If we try to hold on to what's impermanent, feelings of loss and desperation will be a constant part of our lives. In other words, when we fight against what we can't control, we create conflict and tension. In order to experience joy and let go of our grief, we have to accept that people and things will come and go in our lives.

I'm not suggesting that you avoid grief. You know me by now—I would never tell you not to "feel all the feels." Grief is inevitable at some point in your life, but you don't want it to overtake you and rule over you.

I'm also not saying that you have to be detached and unfeeling. You can love someone deeply and not be *attached* to their permanence in your life. The key is acceptance of the cycle of life and death. You will still feel grief, but the sooner you're able to *accept* the inevitable loss of that person, the faster you'll be able to let go of the grief. You might still feel deep sadness, but the pain won't overcome you. It will be pain that changes you in a positive way, not pain that hurts you forever and, thus, changes you negatively. You'll then be able to think fondly about the person you love, and your memories can bring you joy and warmth and comfort.

Impermanence is something we all live with every day. As they say, change is the only thing we can really count on. Even the relationships we have with people who are still with us change all the time. When we stay attached to an ideal about relationships, we run into trouble. If we release our attachment to the way we want the relationship to be from moment to moment, life is a lot easier.

Spread the Love

I release "the idea of the ideal" and let my relationships
be what they are from moment to moment. #YH4M

For example, if I accept that there are days when my husband and I are in bad moods and not getting along well, I'll be able to let the bad days go and remember that there will be good days. No marriage has only great days. We don't have to feel crazy in love with each other every single moment to know that we still do love each other and that the relationship is serving us perfectly. As long as there are more good days than less-than-good ones, there's nothing wrong with our relationship. It works!

Likewise, my relationship with my parents changed through the years. It changed throughout my childhood as I went from being a baby to a school-aged child to a teenager to an adult. And it changed when they left this earth.

Even though they're no longer physically present, I've found that my relationship with my parents continues to change inside me. Many of us have "conversations" with our loved ones after they've passed away. After all, we're usually left with unresolved feelings when someone leaves us. No, a one-sided conversation isn't the same as a conversation with someone who's physically able to talk to you, but those conversations can still help your relationship evolve. Personally, I believe we can communicate to some degree with people who've passed away. I often use meditation to communicate with them, and I even listen for answers that I feel could be coming directly from their energy. (Maybe the conversations aren't so "one-sided" after all.)

But even if that phenomenon is outside your belief system, listening for answers can be productive. You can think of those answers as coming from your own inner wisdom. As long as the messages are nurturing and help you better understand your relationship with your loved one, they're positive.

Releasing Blame

With both of my parents, I felt their energy leave their bodies when they passed. I was touching my father when he passed away, and in that moment, something shifted immediately. I could feel that all the pain we experienced due to our humanness simply no longer existed in the realm where we are pure beings—souls who aren't enmeshed in human drama and tangled in complex psychology.

Still, my father and I'd had a very difficult relationship. He had been through so much during his childhood and never sought healing for it. As a result, he ended up inflicting a lot of pain on our family. Because of that, I found myself gripping tightly to my anger toward him. I thought I "should" feel it. I thought it was only "just" that I stay mad.

Then I had a similar experience with my mother when she passed. I felt her energy leave her body, and I had immediate compassion for her. I knew that everything that had happened between us was the result of her own upbringing, the abusive relationships she had experienced, and the pain she had gone through. She had done the best she could, and I loved her.

I've still had to work hard to release patterns that were created in me as a result of the traumas and pain in my childhood, but I've been able to release much of the blame I felt toward my parents. Meditation has helped me do that. There might be more feelings of blame that come up in the future, and that's perfectly

OK. The task is simply to notice it and use meditation as a tool to let it move through me.

My meditation practice has also helped me accept the rough time my first husband and I experienced during our divorce. As a result of that and the work he's done to heal himself, we've been able to transition into a real friendship. Our relationship is now the healthiest it has ever been—much healthier than it was when we were married. If I had stayed attached to the idea of our being married, unable to let go of that loss, or if I had remained attached to the belief that we were enemies, we never would have come to this place of healing. The fact that my ex and I can communicate in a healthy and positive way today is best for our children, for us, and for our spouses.

My meditation practice has helped me release the need for everything to always be good. I'm better able to allow relationships to go where they need to go and accept that there are lessons to be learned in every experience.

Permanent things in life are the soul, who you are as a person, and the love you feel. That love continues even when someone dies or when a relationship ends. That's what stays with you forever.

Meditation for Releasing Attachment

Preparation / About This Meditation

Attachment almost always leads to sadness because our world is constantly changing. What you attach yourself to—a person, a relationship, a job, or a particular situation or time in your life—can't last forever.

Detaching or unlinking your happiness from things outside of you doesn't indicate a lack of love. You can still love deeply and care wholeheartedly while maintaining healthy autonomy. You can be committed to the success of something without feeling like you can't be happy without it.

I was committed to my first marriage working, but I had to release the idea that being married was attached to my ability to be happy. If I had continued to believe that, I still would be desperately trying to make it work (and failing miserably).

While we're all connected souls sharing a universal experience, our individual happiness has to be found within. Attaching it to anything outside of ourselves leaves us vulnerable to every major and minor event outside of our control.

Of course, this is a much harder concept to accept when talking about the loss of a person and not a situation or material thing, but the truth remains: love is what we are; peace is our natural state. We have little control over what happens outside of our own thoughts, words, and actions, so we must be willing to release attachment to what doesn't belong to us.

This is a meditation for letting go of anything that no longer serves you. It can be an idea, a relationship, a situation, or a feeling. Keep in mind that what doesn't serve you might not be causing you actual harm. You might find that you're attached to something (or someone) that feels good but is ultimately holding you back. A "comfort zone" is an example of something that doesn't look harmful but probably isn't so good for you. You can let go of your attachment to the good stuff, too.

When? I used this meditation often when I was trying to cope with the loss of my parents. It's as much a stress-reducing exercise that eases the physical side effects of attachment as it is a meditation for release. You can practice it several times a day to remind yourself to "let go."

Where? Practice in the safety and comfort of your favorite meditation space or in any quiet place. Speaking your mantras out loud can help amplify the effects of this meditation, so you might want to practice in total privacy.

Position? Sit in your Easy Seat in your meditation space or use the Chair Meditation Pose if sitting cross-legged isn't an option. I practice this meditation at my desk all the time. I've found myself taking part in many debates on social media that don't serve my well-being, and I've had to release my attachment to changing people's minds more than a few times.

You Have 4 Minutes to Release What No Longer Serves You

Let's start with a fill-in-the-blank. "I am ready to let go of _____. It's no longer serving me or the greater good." I can complete that sentence in myriad ways depending on the day. I could release my attachment to a friendship in one moment and my craving for mint chocolate-chip ice cream in the next.

Maybe you're holding on to grief because you've told yourself that letting go means you no longer love the person. I've been there. Maybe you're attached to an idea. I've attached myself to being right and ended up in arguments much longer than necessary. Attachment comes in all shapes and sizes, and letting go of any of it is a step in a positive direction. It's time to release what isn't serving you.

1. Start your meditation by focusing your attention on your breath. Inhale through your nose, and then let go of your exhale with a big, loud "ah" from your mouth. As you inhale and exhale, allow your shoulders to rise and fall, releasing more tension from your physical body with each exhale. Big inhale; "ah" on the exhale. Continue this pattern of breathing for five full breath cycles.

2. Take a moment to recall your fill-in-the-blank statement, and focus on it as you repeat your mantras.

Your Mantra for Letting Go . . .

Use this mantra for quieting your mind, releasing tension, and bringing yourself back to center. Use it inside and outside of your time in meditation. Letting go is a loving gift you give yourself. Accept it with grace.

3. Repeat your mantra either silently or aloud with your eyes closed for ten full breath cycles. You'll recite "let" at the top of each inhale and "go" at the bottom of each exhale. Pause for a moment between breaths to allow for emptiness. Creating energetic space (emptiness) allows your spirit to rest.

You Are a Container for Good . . .

You keep what's good and release what no longer serves you. It's easy for you to let go and move on. What you keep supports your happiness; what you release allows space for peace.

4. Close your eyes and end your practice by repeating the following mantra three times: "I easily release what no longer serves me." When you feel ready, open your eyes and return to your day.

Meditation for Life after Loss

Preparation / About This Meditation

Second only to the gift of life itself is the gift of free will. Each of us has been blessed with the power to make choices that affect the direction of our lives. We are born into circumstances not of our making, but our minds are our own. It's the job of the Universe to present us with challenges, but how we accept each challenge—as a struggle or an opportunity—is completely up to us.

The pain that results from loss is an example of a challenge that can be turned into an opportunity. How we view loss and learn from pain is our choice. Think about the last time you experienced great loss. Did you see it as a slight against you? A punishment? Or did you recognize it as a chance to learn and grow? I'm not suggesting that you view the loss of someone or something you held dear as a blessing, but the gift of being allowed to choose how to react to it certainly is. Every difficulty we survive grows the soul. We become stronger through every tragedy—if it's our will to do so.

We have no option but to move on from pain. Life goes on whether we choose to live in the present moment or not, and making a choice to stay energetically tethered to the past will lead only to suffering. Each present moment becomes an illusion of the past as soon as we enter the next present moment. Are you attached to an illusion and refusing to move on? No matter how crippling you perceive your pain to be, it's your free will to decide between staying stuck in the past and living in the present.

Being changed by pain is also inevitable, but *how* you're changed is a decision left largely up to you. Ignoring the opportunity to be changed for the better by your pain slows your soul's growth and blocks future happiness.

When? Pain can be sharp and unpredictable and also dull and constant. This meditation will serve you in both circumstances. Practice whenever and as often as you need it. It can serve you well to practice this meditation regularly during the period after a great loss.

Where? Any time spent in deep self-reflection can be emotional, but for obvious reasons, this meditation may bring up very intense feelings. Practice in a safe, comfortable, and private space.

Position? A relaxed Easy Seat and Semireclined Bound Angle Pose are both appropriate poses for this meditation. Make sure you feel fully supported in your seat.

Place your hands on your thighs, knees, or to your sides with palms turned up or down. Choose whatever feels most comfortable for you. This may change from practice to practice. You're learning how to connect easily to your intuition, and choosing the perfect positions for your meditations comes naturally for you now.

Practice your Meditation for Life after Loss with your eyes closed when guided, if you can. Open your eyes to read each instruction.

You Have 4 Minutes to Be Changed by Your Pain

Feel safe in this moment knowing that the trauma is over. The painful event is in the past. You have the choice to feel safe, calm, and at peace in this moment. You have already made the loving choice to be here now through this demonstration of self-care.

1. Close your eyes and allow your breath to flow naturally, observing it as it travels from your nostrils, down the back of your throat, fills your chest and your belly, and flows all the way down to your seat. Focus on your breath for ten full breath cycles or until you feel settled and calm in your seat. Then open your eyes for your next instruction.

   It's time to repeat your mantras. It's important that even if you don't believe that your pain is changing you for the better right now, you hold space for the possibility for this to be true.

2. Repeat each of the following two mantras on each exhale of three breath cycles. Pause for a couple of breaths after the first set of breath cycles to open your eyes and read your next mantra. Also take a moment to allow the first mantra to settle just a bit. After your second mantra, open your eyes for your last instruction.

Mantra 1

I choose to *feel* my pain but not be absorbed by it.

Mantra 2

I see and accept the lessons my pain has brought me.

Feel supported in this moment. You are grounded in your seat, and you're completely safe. Be reminded that you've survived every painful event in your life. You are a strong and powerful being, a divine creation, and a vessel for pure love and light.

3. End your meditation with one final mantra. Close your eyes and repeat it three times out loud at the bottom of each of three giant letting-go breaths. Inhale fully; exhale completely. Repeat: "I've changed for the better. I'm powerful in this moment."

Meditation for New Beginnings

Preparation / About This Meditation

I've posted a Meditation for New Beginnings on my YouTube channel every New Year's Eve for the past several years. It's a meditation about letting go and moving on, and it's usually one of my most popular videos of the season.

By the end of any year, I'm pretty anxious to start the next one. The promise of a fresh start is always so exciting to me, no matter what the last year brought me in terms of good or bad. As December winds down and the holidays are neatly packed away in storage boxes and in the corners of my mind, I quickly find myself saying, "Been there, done that. What's next?"

Reflection, goal-setting, and writing statements of release that I burn up in my fireplace mark the start of my new year. But I find myself wanting to hit the reset button at other times of the year, too. Do you make a list of resolutions, and then get frustrated when you're unable to keep them? Do you wish you could just start over again? At the opening of each New Beginnings meditation video, I say something like "This is meant to be a New Year's Meditation, but every day is yours to start brand new." A new beginning can happen at any moment. Remember what I said in your Meditation for Life after Loss: "Each present moment becomes an illusion of the past as soon as we enter the next present moment." Every moment is a blank page, ready for your new story.

A failure isn't the only reason to want to start fresh. You might find yourself ending one phase of life, a relationship, or a situation as you enter another, and you want to make sure that you're leaving behind whatever won't serve you going forward. Good things come to an end, too, and it can be a very positive act to show gratitude for your old situation before moving on. You'll do that during this meditation.

When? Let the first two meditations in this chapter prepare you for this joyful practice of reflection and renewal. Practice this meditation at the end of something—when you've let go and you're ready to move on. Morning is the perfect time for your practice. The start of a new day offers all the possibilities of a clean slate.

Where? Settle into your favorite morning meditation spot. If the sun is out, try to position yourself near a window so that you can bathe yourself in warm sunlight.

Position? Sit up tall in your Easy Seat with your hands resting on your thighs or knees, and your palms upturned. You're setting yourself up to receive new blessings, so make a clear path in your body for energy to flow. Make sure your posture is straight from the crown of your head to your seat, and your shoulders are positioned over your hips.

Open and close your eyes as guided, if you can.

You Have 4 Minutes to Reflect and Renew

Begin your meditation by placing your attention on your easy inhales and exhales as they are in this moment. Allow each inhale to invite a feeling of increased energy and each exhale to release any tension you might be holding. Inhale through your nose, and exhale through your mouth.

1. Read the following message either silently or out loud two times before readying yourself for your

brand-new day: "In this moment, as I let go of something that no longer serves the best and highest good, I also prepare myself for something new and exciting that is guaranteed to come. I celebrate this moment as a time to let go, to move on, and to accept the cycle of life and death of all things. With each inhale and exhale, something begins and something ends, and it's a blessing every time."

2. Close your eyes (or soften the focus of your vision) for ten full breath cycles of energizing inhales and letting-go exhales. Recall the words you just read during this time of quiet contemplation. When you're finished, open your eyes for your sealing mantra.

3. Repeat the following mantra on each exhale of seven breath cycles. After you're finished, continue to breathe with your eyes closed until you feel ready to end your meditation and start your day. Approach your day in the spirit of a radiant warrior, ready to welcome all new challenges, opportunities, and blessings. Your mantra is "This moment is mine to start brand new."

Chapter 10

4 Minutes to Finally Close Emotional and Physical Wounds

When my first son was born, we looked at him and thought, "He's perfect!" Eventually, though, I noticed that he didn't look at me when I nursed him. I knew babies bond with their mothers through eye contact while they nurse. So I made sure to bring it up at his two-month infant checkup.

After the pediatric ophthalmologist examined our sweet baby, we had a diagnosis—ocular albinism. This genetic condition is a type of albinism that affects only the eyes. The irises and retinas of the eyes don't have enough pigment, so vision is impaired—sometimes severely.

"There's no treatment for OA except risky experimental possibilities," the doctor told us. "It doesn't get worse, but it also doesn't get better. It means that he may be very close to blind his whole life. Your son might not be able to ride a bike, and he'll probably never drive a car. He won't be able to play sports, and he may have to walk with a cane."

It was a scary diagnosis. Google wasn't yet what it is now, so looking up OA required navigating primitive search engines, digging through message boards, and taking trips to the library. Would our son be OK? Would we be able to handle his needs? Yet, in the middle of all the fear, when I looked at my baby, all I could see was perfection. Others might label him as "disabled" or "blind" or "imperfect," but we've never treated him like that.

Right away I became his advocate, and it was clear to me that he would only be limited if we saw him as limited. As long as we saw him as a perfect, divine creation, I knew he'd be able to do whatever he wanted in life to make himself happy.

As a result, he's growing up to not only be an athlete in several sports (even ice hockey!) but also he has never needed a cane to walk. He's an artist and an incredibly talented musician. He rides a bike just fine, thank you very much—even though the only line on the eye chart that he can read is the first one, the big *E* at the top. He might never be able to drive a car, but he's far from a disabled person. His abilities outshine any of his so-called challenges.

And I've seen the same success in my younger son, who was also diagnosed with OA shortly after he was born. He, too, can do many of the things we were told he'd never be able to do. We've seen other kids with the same diagnosis and visual acuity walking with canes and unable to ride bikes or participate in sports.

How we perceive "afflictions" or "illnesses" or "emotional wounds" can make a world of difference in how they affect us. I've seen that firsthand with my sons, and they've been great teachers for me in dealing with my own physical and emotional wounds. Their diagnoses are real. The fact that they don't see as well as people with normal vision can't be denied. But their reactions to their diagnoses make them remarkable. Whatever physical limitations they have won't be further impaired by a negative mind-set. They push their limits every day, guaranteeing personal excellence.

My boys have shown me that they are, I am, and you are whole people who were created the way we were on purpose—regardless of anything that has happened to any of us.

Uncovering the Purpose of Wounds

Not only are we whole people who were created on purpose, but we're whole people created *with* purpose, as we talked about in Chapter 7. We tend to think of purpose as what we're supposed to *do* with our lives, and, yes, it's great when we can express our purpose in some way in the world—especially if it becomes a profession or a means of helping others. But searching for our purpose brings up all kinds of anxieties. We're instructed by gurus and guidance counselors—people who want the best for us—to keep "looking" for our purpose. Where is it? Is it over there? Or maybe it's in the opposite direction?

After participating in a panel discussion with my colleague, author Alexandra Jamieson, I began seeing purpose in an entirely different way. She said we need to get rid of the idea of "looking for" our purpose. When we use the words *find* or *look,* we search outside of ourselves. But our purpose actually lies within us. So she suggests replacing *look* and *find* with *uncover.* As soon as she said that, a lightbulb went on in my head. I visualized a glowing light at my heart center, and I saw an image of my chest opening and the layers peeling away to reveal the truth of who I really am. It completely changed the way I view this concept of "purpose."

When I peel away the layers of fear and conditioning that have built up from the emotional and physical wounds in my life, I have the ability to find that purpose underneath. If we look at the concept of purpose beyond simply what we're meant to "do," we see that everything has a purpose—a seed of opportunity that, when nurtured, provides insight into divine intention.

So if I look at my sons' ocular albinism from that perspective and remove the stigma of the word *disability,* underneath it is a beautiful purpose. We might not be able to pinpoint what that purpose is exactly, but that doesn't matter. I trust the divine intention behind their diagnoses. And that helps me to see both of them as whole and not at all disabled.

They're living their lives of purpose, and like everyone, they have certain challenges that teach them the lessons they're meant to learn. Think about it: We all do some things better than others. Some of us are good at math, while others of us are great with words or with our hands. Some of us can draw very well, and others of us can sing or dance. Some of us have trick knees, are pigeon-toed, or have stiff necks that get in the way of some activities. None of us can do absolutely everything. Why should we call anything a *disability*? It's only when we dwell on what we can't do well that we have a problem. When we use what we have and stop focusing on what we don't have, we stay connected to our wholeness and to our purpose.

Outlook, perspective, and mind-set make all the difference. No, neither of my sons walk around with phony Pollyanna attitudes, saying, "It's *so* great that I can't see!" But they also don't walk around saying, "Woe is me. Everybody else can see, and I can't." Nor do they say, "How am I going to be successful in spite of this?" Theirs is a practical outlook even more than a positive outlook. They say, "How am I going to be successful *using* this?"

Remember: even our pain, both physical and emotional, has important lessons for us that we can use if we choose.

Spread the Love

Healing comes when I understand that my pain has a purpose.
#YH4M

PAIN IS A BIRTH PROCESS

One of the core teachings that I use as a doula for women during childbirth is that their pain is there to serve them. When we see pain as something that serves us and reveals something valuable, we begin to relax, and the pain begins to ease. In childbirth, it's very easy to see how the pain has served us because what's revealed is a new baby, presented to us "earth-side."

When women in childbirth let go of their resistance to their pain and ease their fear, they have a much easier birth experience.

The same holds true for whatever kind of pain we're experiencing, whether it's illness, "disability," trauma, or heartbreak. When we accept that there's a purpose for the pain and that it's serving us in some way—even if we don't yet know how—we allow good things to happen. We give birth to something new.

Destiny vs. Divine Intention

When we think about purpose, we often equate it with "destiny"—something that's meant to happen, something predestined. With my Christian background, I always found destiny to be a difficult concept to wrap my head around. Does God really know our future? Does that mean there's no free will? No ability to change our course? The idea of that made me feel helpless and out of control. So, over time, I moved toward and accepted the concept of divine intention.

With divine intention, we're participants in what happens in our lives. We can evolve and learn and change our direction. When I look around at my own life and the lives of those around me, that's what I see taking place.

In my experience, prayer and meditation are the best ways to keep us connected to divine intention—the best ways to bring ourselves back to grace. We get stuck and lose our ability to move forward when we deviate from divine intention or stop connecting through meditation or prayer.

Spread the Love

I'm a partner with the Divine in bringing myself back to grace.
#YH4M

There's a woman in my private yoga group on Facebook who, despite her best efforts, has continued to have painful experiences. She's done all the things that have been suggested to her, but her life hasn't changed for the better. "Why am I stuck being broke?" she asked me. "Why do I keep getting the short end of the stick?"

Over and over again, she characterized the challenges that came into her life as "bad," instead of seeing the lesson, the service, the gift, and the purpose in each experience. She was disconnected from the Divine because she saw her experiences as bad luck or even as punishment. She felt jinxed.

If she could begin to peel back the layers and uncover the purpose in each experience, she would be able to connect again with the Divine. Or if she could at least come to a place of accepting that divine intention is at work, it would make a big difference for her. The energy would shift. Then the pattern would begin to let go and allow her to move forward. If we use the birth analogy again, when we disconnect from the purpose in our experiences, it's almost like refusing the birth. We don't allow the new to come forth.

Sometimes we hold on to the pain. We see ourselves as being tolerant of pain, and that can block us from receiving the lesson. We say, "I'm tough," and we build up a resistance to pain. But that resistance to pain also makes us resistant to what we could learn from it. When we toughen up, we ignore the lesson in the pain. When we accept that the Divine has a purpose in what we're experiencing, the pain eases. We don't have to toughen up so much. The pain may not go away entirely, but it won't have as much power over us.

This concept is nothing new, of course. It's the ancient concept of karma. Until we learn the lesson, we're forced to repeat it. Understanding is what unlocks the pattern and sets us free. We're then able to honor whatever we're going through in the moment. We can remove the stigma—"bad," "disability," "tragedy"—that we attach to it. We can begin to reframe it and see that at the heart of it is the glowing light of purpose.

The Blessing in the Breaking

In Chapter 9 we talked about how pain can hurt you or change you. We can accept the hurt, but then we have to decide how it's going to change us for the better. Even when working out with a muscle, the muscle has to be broken down a bit in order for it to grow. A bodybuilder sees blessing in the soreness after a workout because that's the best indicator that something good is happening. They know that when they're sore, they're going to see growth. The hurt is changing them for the better. When we see our physical and emotional pain as an exercise in growth, the pain immediately eases, the birth begins, and the healing starts.

Bishop T. D. Jakes has a sermon based on the loaves and fishes, in which he talks about how the real lesson in those verses of the Bible is that the *blessing comes in the breaking*. When there wasn't enough bread, and the bread was broken, the blessing happened.

When you feel like your heart is breaking apart, it's actually breaking open and revealing the blessing. We allow for so much more after the breaking!

Think of it this way: "Light is in both the broken bottle and the diamond." This quote from Mark Nepo shows us that, like my sons, what appears to be broken is actually whole and valuable.

Society sees diamonds as perfect and beautiful. We think of them as rare, even though they're not. We decided that they're the best rock for no other reason than we simply decided it. But something as common as a discarded piece of broken glass that you might find on a dirt road has the very same ability as a diamond to reflect light and all the beautiful colors of the rainbow.

This is a perfect analogy for when we look at ourselves as broken. If you think you have less of an ability to heal than others, less of an ability to create change in your life, or less ability to connect with the Divine, think of that broken glass. Whatever has caused the breaking has helped create the many facets of your personality, and you are no less shiny than a diamond.

Some people might see my sons as broken bottles, but that doesn't matter because their ability to shine and reflect light is the same as a diamond. Their ability to reflect the light is the same as people with 20/20 vision.

It's our choice to see ourselves as broken or whole. To me, seeing ourselves as broken is a lie we tell ourselves out of fear. My sons have taught me that. For me, the light in a broken bottle is proof that we're already whole. Ironically, the breaking helps us to recognize that wholeness and bring it into the light.

While unbroken bottles and uncut diamonds can reflect light to some degree, it's the cuts that allow them to reflect light the most. That's why the cut of a diamond is so cherished. Human beings are the same. When the breaking happens to us, the layers of conditioning and fears that cover our purpose begin to fall away. The breaking is what forces us to peel back the layers, look within, and reveal the beauty of who we really are. The breaking cracks us open so that the light of our true selves is revealed. Remember that even diamonds have to be cut, shaped, and polished to reveal their hidden beauty.

So the breaking can actually be welcome if we let it. The breaking helps us access the tools we need, and a primary function of those tools is simply seeing the breaking for what it really is. That's when we start to develop our strength, when our wisdom grows, when we learn to care for ourselves better, and when we see that part of self-care is the acceptance of the challenges life brings us. We develop more tools so that the next break is just a little bit easier.

My boys have developed amazing coping skills. They have an answer ready every time someone comes up to them and asks, "Why do your eyes look funny?" or "Why are your eyes shaking back and forth?" They're prepared with a protection in their heart that says, "This is my lesson and part of my purpose. I'm not only meant to find the light inside of me, but I'm also meant to shine light so that others can learn." Teaching other people helps them love and accept themselves more fully. When they explain ocular albinism to other people, the words they use are very important. They break it down in simple terms so that others understand that it's really no big deal. Some people are tall; some are short. Some people see; others don't. My sons teach us how to understand and accept ourselves as we are.

I'm not trying to pretend that the wounds we experience are easy. Far from it. But they can be *less difficult* if we allow them to be. I find that in my life, I need to constantly remind myself that the blessing is in the breaking. When the breaking happens, I try to open up and allow as much love as possible to flow into me. Then I have the strength to grow and peel back the layers fully to reveal the purpose of the breaking. And if the purpose and the lesson are still hazy to my intellect, I remind myself to trust in divine intention and have faith that there *is* a higher purpose—an opportunity to learn—whether I can see it or not.

How Meditation Helps Heal Our Wounds

I had Lyme disease for a long time, and it was a difficult healing process. But even though relapses are possible, that was an impermanent wound, impermanent pain. For my sons, unless some cure comes along during their lifetimes, their ocular albinism is permanent. Heartbreak, divorce, and loss are all impermanent wounds, but there's a permanent residue that remains. That residue is part of the process of the breaking. We can think of that residue as some awful damage that we have to live with, or we can think of it as no more than facets of the broken glass—facets of our wholeness that reflect light.

It's when we fear that our heartbreak or illness will happen again or when we have a stigma attached to it—such as a judgment about divorce, "disability," or "damage"—that we fight against the pain. That's when we're no longer aligned with divine intention, and the facets of the glass become obscured by shadows.

I'm not saying that you have to be superhuman and never feel pain. It's natural to experience pain and fall into feeling as though you're damaged or broken. But that's exactly why a meditation practice is so important. Meditation helps us ease our fears surrounding pain and repeatedly realign ourselves with divine intention and purpose. For me it has been a lifeline through the many moments of breaking in my life.

Meditation also allows us to become the observer and to develop greater compassion for ourselves. Judgments are difficult to let go of when we're in pain. Sometimes we feel that we brought on our wounds by making mistakes that warrant punishment. We believe we deserve what happened to us. As a mother it was easy for me to see my sons as perfect, whole beings—even with their diagnoses. We know that the illnesses and heartbreaks of others don't define them, but it's harder for us to see that our own illnesses and heartbreaks don't define us either. It takes regular meditation for me to be able to see myself with the same level of tolerance, acceptance, and love that I have for my children.

Remember: we're still whole, no matter what mistakes we've made or what has happened to us. Our experiences are things we have; they're not who we are.

Meditation also reminds us that who we are in this moment has nothing to do with who we will be in the next. Even an illness constantly changes and evolves. It's an energetic entity that no more stays the same than we do. So we can choose to let go of the pain—or at least how we think about the pain. We can choose to see ourselves as broken or whole. Each moment is an opportunity to start again—to be brand new. It's a gift every single time.

I use the mantra "No matter where I've been, who I've been, or what I've done, this moment is mine to make everything brand new. I'm not defined by my past. Regret can never serve me. I'm energized by the potential in every moment." Again, when we repeat a mantra in meditation, we begin to believe it. And then we start to live it.

We can put aside what happened before. We can see the beauty in the breaking, allow for growth, and invite each moment to fully serve us.

As you've already learned, you can also ask questions of yourself in meditation and listen quietly for answers. You can ask, "How can this illness, disability, or challenge be my teacher?" Remind yourself to stay patient if the answer doesn't come right away. Keep asking. Once again, approach your pain with curiosity rather than judgment. Getting quiet and listening to yourself while in a state of peace and calm will give you the opportunity to get answers that can heal you.

We all deserve to feel healthy, happy, and light. Illness, heartbreak, and all the traumas that happen in our lives are about being broken open so that we can reveal our true beauty within. It's our job to observe the pieces from the breaking—picking up only the pieces that serve us and reflect light, using what we have available to us to evolve into the essence of who we really are. That evolution toward our true selves is the key to a happier life that allows us to finally close our physical and emotional wounds.

Meditation for Finding Purpose in Pain

Preparation / About This Meditation

This is not a meditation for welcoming more pain into your life. No matter how grateful I am for the lessons my pain has taught me, you'll never find me praying for more. Thanks, God— I'm good with what I've got!

What this meditation *will* do is help you to accept the pain you've already experienced or are experiencing now as a valuable teacher in your life. It can also help to reduce your fear about pain that hasn't yet come—both random and predictable. Pain from a sudden breakup, injury, or death can come without warning, and that's pain that we deal with after it's arrived. We can prepare ourselves for pain that's attached to predictable events like childbirth, losing someone after a terminal illness, and divorce.

Pain can break us, but it doesn't ruin us. Even a broken bottle is still a bottle. It just looks a little different. Breaking transforms us. That's the beautiful purpose of pain. The period of transformation is when we get to learn and grow from the breaking, and the breaking reveals the blessing.

You've already learned that I'm an unapologetic fan of reality TV. I was watching Caitlyn Jenner recount her experience of telling her children about what it meant to be transgender. She explained that while she's different, she's not broken. God didn't make a mistake by trapping a woman's brain inside a man's body. God doesn't make mistakes—there is only divine intention. Caitlyn was created with extraordinary capabilities that allowed her to win Olympic medals and create successful businesses. She was also created with some other qualities that would challenge her and sometimes feel like they were breaking her. The Universe sets us up for success, but we have to see our challenges—our pain— as opportunities for success. Caitlyn was a whole person—created with divine intention—even through periods of confusion, pain, heartache, and breaking. What was revealed after her period of pain turned out to be some of her greatest blessings.

When? You can practice this meditation at any time of the day. Use it in the midst of heartache or after your painful event has passed.

Where? Choose a private space for your meditation, or practice in your regular spot. I prefer to practice this meditation in total silence or with as little noise distraction as possible. You can make an exception for sounds of nature, as they're always a beautiful reminder of our place in the Universe.

Position? Sit in a relaxed Easy Seat with your hands resting gently on your lap in Cup/Chalice Mudra. As you may recall, this mudra is indicated for balancing energy in your body. I always feel an increased sensation of support and also connection to self when I use this mudra.

It's best to spend most of this meditation with your eyes closed, if you can. Open them to read the instructions when guided.

You Have 4 Minutes to Discover the Gifts in Misfortune

"The blessing is in the breaking, and there is light in the broken bottle." This combination of two of my favorite quotes makes my heart sing with excitement. The breaking that has happened to you is an opportunity to reveal all your glorious potential. And the shattered pieces that remain reflect the light of a million sparkling diamonds.

1. Focus your attention on your breath. Take a moment to acknowledge the fact that you're here and that your breath is a blessing. Welcome each inhale with a silent thank-you. Allow each exhale to exit your body without any effort. Just let it flow.

2. Close your eyes and follow your natural inhales and exhales for ten full breath cycles, allowing each breath to fill and empty. Fill and empty. Your breath flows evenly and effortlessly. When you're finished, open your eyes for your next step.

You're Ready to Receive Your Message . . .

3. Now that you're completely calm and settled into your meditation, it's time to receive your message. Read the following message either silently or aloud three times. Take the time to read it slowly, paying careful attention to each word. "As my heart breaks, it opens itself to love and new opportunities. The pieces of my shattered spirit are blessings, and they are beautiful. Light reflects and shines from the pieces of my shattered spirit."

4. Close your eyes and continue to follow your long, easy breaths for ten more breath cycles. Allow the words you just read to settle into every cell of your body. Open your eyes after your tenth inhale and exhale to read your final instruction.

Inspire a Deeper Love . . .

5.   Close your eyes and repeat your mantra either silently or aloud at the bottom of each exhale for five breath cycles. Accept these words as true. Allow them to inspire a deeper feeling of respect for your journey and love for yourself as you are right now. When you're finished, take one last deep breath, smile big, and return to your day. "The blessing is in the breaking. My light is revealed."

Meditation for Healing

Preparation / About This Meditation

The healing process is a wonderful, awe-inspiring phenomenon not to be discounted as anything less. I regularly "nerd out" over things like protective scabs forming over scrapes and how the body makes natural anesthesia during childbirth. Our bodies and the spirits that occupy them are miraculous creations capable of self-healing.

Tools like modern and ancient medicine, meditation, and prayer are also integral to the healing process. We can do much to prevent illness and injury and also to aid healing. Your time spent in meditation can help reduce stress and ease emotional and physical suffering. Of course, you should always consult with your professional health-care provider before treating any medical condition.

Your Meditation for Healing will give you the opportunity to experiment with visualization to help ease emotional and physical pain. I'm also going to guide you through a physical exercise to help move energy through your body. Don't worry! I'm not talking about a workout. This whole meditation can be performed in the comfort of your preferred posture.

When? Any time of day is appropriate for this meditation. If you're struggling with pain that makes performing regular daily tasks difficult, morning might work best. If you need help feeling comfortable enough to fall asleep, practice this meditation in the evening right before bed.

I mentioned before that I often struggle with the long-term physical effects of Lyme disease. I use the techniques in this meditation at bedtime to help ease pain in my joints and muscles.

Where? Practice your healing meditation in a comfortable, quiet space. This is a meditation best reserved for home or another place where you feel completely relaxed.

Position? Easy Seat and Semireclined Bound Angle Pose both complement this meditation well. You might also like to try Corpse Pose, which would allow you to be fully reclined. Whichever pose you choose, make sure that you feel completely comfortable and fully supported.

If in Easy Seat, place your hands on your thighs or knees with your palms upturned; if in Semireclined Bound Angle Pose or Corpse Pose, place your hands at your sides. Toward the end of your meditation, I'll guide you to use your hands in an exercise to move healing energy through your body. You can return your hands to their original position after the exercise.

This meditation contains more instruction than most of the others, so your eyes will be open during much of it. Close your eyes during the visualization exercise and when guided.

You Have 4 Minutes to Heal Yourself

You're about to send healing light to every part of your body. You will feel warmed and comforted by this light. Prepare yourself for relaxation and rejuvenation as you settle into your chosen pose.

1. As you bring your attention to your easy inhales and exhales, and settle yourself into your comfortable,

supportive pose, close your eyes and start to imagine a glowing, white orb of light floating above your head. This light expands and contracts with every inhale and exhale, and it bounces joyfully as your body rises and falls ever so slightly with each breath. Focus your attention on this light right above your head for ten full breath cycles before opening your eyes for your next step.

2. Now imagine the glowing orb entering your body at the crown of your head and slowly making its way down and through your body, filling you with white light. Light travels to every part of your body, and you're glowing with radiant energy.

Send Light to Your Pain . . .

3. Whatever discomfort you feel in this moment— whether emotional or physical—is about to receive the healing warmth of your white light. Close your eyes and repeat the following mantra either silently or aloud on the exhale of five breath cycles. See your light form a glowing orb once again and travel straight to the location of your pain. If you're experiencing heartache, send your light to your heart center.

Mantra 1

I send healing light to my pain.

4. Allow your orb to grow and fill your entire body once again. Close your eyes and repeat your second mantra on the exhale of five breath cycles.

Mantra 2

I am safe and in perfect health.

Light has traveled to every part of your body, warming you and providing gentle relief from your pain. Imagine your pain as being burnt up by your healing light, with only ashes remaining as evidence of its existence. It's time to "clean up" these ashes with a few gentle strokes of your hands.

5. With your eyes open or closed, run your right hand from your left shoulder down your left arm, all the way over and past the fingertips of your left hand, and say, "I release my pain to the Universe."

6. Now run your left hand from your right shoulder down your right arm, all the way over and past the fingertips of your right hand, and repeat, "I release my pain to the Universe."

7. Place both hands on your upper thighs near your hip creases with palms turned down. Run your palms down your legs, past your knees, and repeat, "I release my pain to the Universe."

8. Choose one hand and place it over your heart. Sweep your hand up toward your face, past your chin, and repeat, "I release my pain to the Universe."

9. Take the same hand, and place it over your forehead. Sweep your hand up toward the sky and repeat, "I release my pain to the Universe."

   All remnants of your pain have been swept away and released to the Universe. Your burden has been lessened as the Universe has agreed to support your healing process.

10. Take a few moments to close your eyes and rest. Allow your attention to travel back to your breath.

See your body glow with your healing, white light.
Enjoy this time of relief for as long as feels good.
When you feel ready, open your eyes and return to
the outside world.

Meditation for Strength

Preparation / About This Meditation

Why is it that when we survive trauma, we label ourselves
as "damaged"? We're alive and making it through the day, albeit
sometimes with a little difficulty, but making it from sunup till
sundown all the same. Yet we're walking around telling ourselves
and other people that we're not good enough. If you're doing this,
stop it. Stop it right now, and get ready to hear some truth.

You haven't been *damaged* by what's happened to you. You've
been *strengthened*. In every moment, with every breath, the Universe has been strengthening you for your path. You're ready for
whatever's coming your way because you've survived battle. You're
a warrior.

Like you, I've been through some stuff. And while my stuff
isn't your stuff, we can all relate to having stuff. But our stuff
doesn't have to be baggage that weighs us down. It can be gleam-
ing armor that protects our hearts and shines brilliantly for all to
see. Your armor tells the world, "Look at me! I'm a mighty warrior
for love, and I can teach you how to be one, too. I'm not damaged.
I'm a divine creation, worthy of all the good the Universe has
to offer!"

Just like love doesn't exist only in the total absence of fear,
strength doesn't exist only in the total absence of weakness, insecurity, or self-doubt. We can feel tired or afraid *and* feel strong.
There have been days of heartache when even getting out of bed
and brushing my teeth felt like a monumental task, but I knew
that I had been given the strength to do it. On those days, I told
myself, "You're strong enough for just one step. And now another.
And another. You've been given this moment for a reason. Take

the step. Move forward. What's done is done. This moment is yours to choose to be alive."

When? I love practicing this meditation in the morning. It readies me for my day and inspires me to approach every battle—big or small—with the mind-set of a peaceful warrior.

Where? Practice in your favorite meditation space, on the bus or train during your morning commute, in your car before you walk into work, or wherever feels good. By now you're a champion of meditation. You can meditate anywhere!

Position? Sit up tall in Easy Seat, feeling and looking strong in your posture. Inhale your shoulders up to your ears, and then roll your shoulder blades back and down along your spine a couple of times to make sure your chest is nice and open.

Place your hands on your thighs or knees with palms upturned or in Kubera Mudra.

Close your eyes while practicing visualization or reciting your mantras, or keep them open with your vision focused on a single object.

You Have 4 Minutes to Take Charge of Your Pain

Dear Warrior: You are ready. Everything you've done, everything you've seen, and everything that has been done to you has prepared you for this moment. You have survived because you're strong.

You're about to light up your body with pure energy channeled from the Universe. You are a force of nature.

1. Begin your meditation with five deep, cleansing breaths. Each breath will awaken your senses, fill you with energy, and release all tension from your body. Inhale deeply and feel your entire body fill with air. Let everything go with your exhale. With each

breath, your energy increases, and you release any tension you're holding. Inhale; feel your whole body expand. Exhale; let go.

2. Now focus your attention on your seat. Feel your body connected to the surface beneath you. Close your eyes for just a few breaths as you examine your connection to the physical surface, then the energetic vibration of the earth below. Imagine yourself connected energetically through the floor, the ground, and the layers of earth beneath. Imagine a column of energy passing from the crown of your head, through your body, and reaching all the way down to the earth's core.

   From the base of your seat to the crown of your head, your chakras are represented by each color of the rainbow: red, orange, yellow, green, blue, indigo, and violet. You're going to wake up your chakras, creating a clear channel for energy to flow. The column of energy I mentioned will flow freely through your body, connecting you with both the light of the Universe and the fiery power of the earth's core. This flow of energy will provide you with incredible strength—both physical and spiritual.

   Before closing your eyes, read the following descriptions for each of the seven chakra stations in your body. Then, with your eyes closed, follow the path of your chakras from your seat to your crown. You're going to focus on each chakra for the length of three full breath cycles. When you've finished visiting each chakra, open your eyes to read your next step.

3. Starting with your Root Chakra (at your base or pelvic floor), imagine a red, glowing light that expands and contracts with each inhale and exhale. After three breaths, move on to your Sacral Chakra (lower

abdomen), glowing orange. Visit your Solar Plexus Chakra (in your belly), which is bright yellow like the sun. Your Heart Chakra is next, glowing with a vibrant, emerald green. Your light blue Throat Chakra pulsates with life and allows your true voice to break free. You arrive at your indigo Third Eye Chakra and feel wisdom and loving thought passing through. Ending at your Crown Chakra, hovering above your head with a brilliant, violet hue, you feel a powerful channel of spiritual knowledge, insight, and love connecting you to the entire Universe.

Cleansed, Renewed, and Powerful . . .

4. Read the following message out loud two times: "No matter where I've been, who I've been, or what I've done, this moment is mine to make everything brand new. No matter what has happened to me, it doesn't define who I am. I was created whole, and I'm a whole person no matter what. I am a partner with the Divine in bringing myself back to grace."

5. Close your eyes and continue to breathe deeply. You might notice that your breaths are longer, deeper, and clearer. You feel energized and alive! Observe your inhales and exhales, and witness how you feel even more powerful with each breath cycle. When you're ready, open your eyes, and go forth to conquer your day.

Chapter 11

4 Minutes to Cultivate Gratitude, Abundance, and Service

I've found in my life that gratitude, abundance, and service form a circle that keeps me in perfect alignment with my purpose. Here's how it works: I make a conscious effort to be grateful for all that I have, and this gratitude opens me up to receive more abundance. As I experience more abundance, I want to share my riches and be of service to others. The joy of providing service ignites even more gratitude in me, which opens me up to more abundance, which then provides me with more opportunities and more impetus to provide service. And the circle keeps turning.

The service we provide ignites gratitude in others, too, which helps them open to receive abundance and makes them want to be of service as well. It's a lot like the paying-it-forward and random-acts-of-kindness movements. Can you see the beauty of this circle? Each of the three aspects of the circle feeds the other.

Note that by abundance, I'm not talking just about money. I'm talking about abundant health, abundant friends, abundant happiness, abundant peace—all the good things in life.

Let's talk about how you can welcome each of the three aspects of the circle into your life. Then you'll meditate on each and enter this beautiful circle of infinite blessings.

Gratitude

Cultivating gratitude is an action that you have to consciously take. It's a nonnegotiable in my life because I truly believe that I can't experience joy without being grateful.

If I can't feel grateful for what I have, I can't welcome more into my life. Some teachers will tell you that we shouldn't wish for more. But I'm not talking about greed. I'm talking about the natural human desire for more of what nurtures our happiness. We don't look at a clear, blue sky and say, "Well, that's enough of that!" We want more of it, and no one would ever blame you for saying, "I want more blue skies." So why limit other abundance in your life? Don't feel guilty about wanting more or having more. When you have more, you get to share more with others. Each and every one of us has a life that deserves to shine brighter.

Spread the Love

My life deserves to shine brighter. When I allow myself to have more, it gives me more to share with others. #YH4M

There's a New Testament Bible verse in the book of Luke that says, "He that is faithful in that which is least is faithful also in much." My friend and motivational speaker Danny-J. introduced me to this quote by telling me to "be faithful in the little things." This message was given to her by one of her mentors. All it means is that it's imperative to show appreciation for the things we normally take for granted—little things like indoor plumbing.

Remember that a lot of people in the world don't have it. When we can see and appreciate what we have rather than focus on what we don't have, we open the door for more to come to us.

Let's say I have just enough money to pay my bills. A good start is to say, "I'm grateful," but I can take it a step further and say, "I have all that I need to support myself in this moment, and I'm grateful." Even when I had to use my credit cards to pay for food, transportation, and clothing, I made sure I showed my gratitude: "I have credit to buy necessities, and I'm grateful."

You might have just enough food to sustain you in this moment, but when you say, "I have all that I need, and I'm grateful," you're speaking the truth because you're still alive right now. This expression of sincere gratitude gives the Universe a cue that you're responsible and faithful. You honor what you have, and that brings you greater possibility of a windfall. That's certainly been true in my life.

Spread the Love

In being grateful, I welcome abundance. #YH4M

I see this phenomenon everywhere in my life now. When I was struggling with my finances and couldn't cover my bills, there was virtually nothing different about my circumstances than there is today. I had access then to everything I have access to now. The change that was required was, as they say, an "inside job." I had to overcome my fears and self-esteem issues. I had to understand that I'm worthy and created with divine intention. I didn't have to make many changes to my outside world. You'll notice that in this book, I haven't taught you how to write a résumé to get the job of your dreams or an online dating profile to find the love of your life.

That's because wherever you are right now, you probably have all you need to feel many moments of happiness and experience success. Now, I do realize that there might be real obstacles in your life. You might be in a relationship with someone who doesn't support you, or you might be working at a job you hate. Even though these are physical situations that you might need to find a way to leave, that action starts from the inside. The mantras and meditations are what give you the courage to change and to feel deserving of a better life. They help you realize that more is possible for you. And they give you the inner power to move out of your current circumstances without undeserved feelings of regret.

It's also true that the more you remain faithful in the little things—what you already have right now—the faster you'll experience that transformation.

GRATITUDE JOURNALING

Gratitude journaling is something I do every single day before I meditate. When I wake up in the morning, I find three things to say "thank you" for. I started out just saying the three things out loud. Then I began to write them down. I've found that the act of writing imprints the gratitude onto my conscious mind for the day ahead. And then I go into my meditation practice. Sometimes I just contemplate my gratitude in meditation. Other times I do one of the mantras from this book. But whatever mantra I choose, it starts with the gratitude practice.

I encourage you to do your gratitude journaling as soon as you wake up—even before you get out of bed or brush your teeth, if possible. You can write down what you're grateful for in a notebook, on your phone, on your tablet—wherever you like. But keep it on your nightstand within easy reach.

Yes, it's a struggle some days to think of even three things to be grateful for, especially when we're going through something difficult. But even so, gratitude serves as a "balancing." It isn't even about having gratitude for the obvious things like a roof over your head or your family. Look for the tiniest things that are easily overlooked.

My practice is to find the most insignificant thing that I could be grateful for during my day—faith in the little things. Maybe it's the post office clerk who, the day before, asked how my kids were doing. Maybe it's the person who waved me on in traffic so that I didn't have to wait for a long line of cars to pass. Maybe it was finding my favorite kind of pistachios on sale. We usually overlook these things because of the very real problems that we deal with on a day-to-day basis. But those small moments really do make our lives better—and yes, happier.

My gratitude practice creates balance in my life and offers me new perspective. We crave balance, which we think means an even amount of one thing versus another. But balance is really about seeing that it isn't all bad—even if it feels all bad. We can balance reality against our perception, and we do that by finding happiness where it truly exists—inside of ourselves and in the small, ordinary moments of life.

Abundance

One of the interesting "laws" about abundance is that it begets itself. The more I receive, the more I get comfortable with the feeling of deserving. Then the ceiling continues to rise.

Dr. Wayne W. Dyer once talked about the checks that showed up in his mailbox on a regular basis. He didn't even know where they had come from. At first I thought, "That sounds awful! I wouldn't feel comfortable getting checks like that. I wouldn't feel like I'd worked for them."

That just goes to show how much work I needed to do on my feelings of deserving! Who thumbs their nose at easy money? Not this girl—not anymore. Now, like Wayne, I'm also getting royalty checks. They aren't as direct as "work this many hours and get a check for this much money," but they're certainly a result of the work I've done. It's what we call "passive income." Since I've improved my feelings of deserving, I welcome these checks as a reward for all that time I remained faithful when I had very little.

Besides financial abundance, my meditation practice has helped me create abundance in relationships. I already talked about the wonderful women friends and mentors who have come into my life. My marriage is also gigantic proof to me that I have opened up to the love I deserve in this life.

Now, I'm not saying that if you don't have a romantic relationship, it means you're not believing enough in how much you deserve. It could be that working on worthiness will open you up to attracting a partner, but we all have our own path when it comes to romance. What I do know for sure is that the more you work on your sense of self-worth, the more love you will receive, whether it's romantic love, friendship, or familial love. You'll never have to worry about getting all the love you need in order to thrive.

I have also discovered that when I accept my body as it is, I have better health. When I accepted my body with its stretch marks, saggy parts, and bumpy parts—including the acknowledgment that it could be stronger and healthier—it did get stronger, healthier, and even more attractive. Even if you have health challenges, express gratitude for where your body is today. Then accept and allow for improvement.

There are opportunities for gratitude in every area of your life if you just look!

Service

As I said in Chapter 7, our shared purpose is to love and to be loved, and to learn and to teach. Teaching is loving—it's all connected. All these gifts that we've been given are so that we can be of service by sharing our growth and learning with others.

What does service look like? It can be expressed in so many ways. It's me writing this book, teaching my children the lessons I've learned, helping a friend emotionally or financially because I have the time or money to give, or donating time or resources to charity. It's buying my daughter a copy of *Be Here Now* when she turned 15, the same age I was when I stole the book from my mother's friend's bookstore—a full-circle legacy of learning that I could pass on to her and help her open to spirituality. (And the ability to *buy* the book with my well-earned money is not lost on me as an opportunity to express gratitude.)

Service can also be as small as smiling at a stranger, holding a door open for someone, or saying "thank you" to someone who doesn't ordinarily get a thank-you—such as the gas station attendant, the customer service representative, or the bus driver.

The circle of gratitude, abundance, and service must fulfill itself. Some people cut off the circle by cultivating gratitude and welcoming the abundance but never sharing in service. If you cut off the service part, you get stuck. The flow is blocked and you'll cease to have abundance flow back to you.

To keep the flow of abundance going, it's imperative that you make room for more, and you do that by creating space. You can create space for more only when you let go and pass it on . . . or pay it forward, as the phrase goes.

So much of what I've written about in this book involves creating space. When I wrote about fear as a big ball of mystery, I talked about how you make the fear smaller and create more space for courage and confidence by asking questions about the fear. When we let go of feelings of attachment, we make space for love to move in. That's what happened to me when I was able to stop being so clingy with my husband. Suddenly there was more space, both between us in our relationship and inside me in my relationship with myself. This space allowed me to receive more love from my husband, family, and friends.

By finding what works for me in my meditation practice and sharing it with others like you, I complete the circle of gratitude, abundance, and service. I then feel gratitude for the ability to bring something to you that I hope will help you in your life and inspire you to help others. And the circle continues.

So, as change happens for you, go out and spread your light in the way that feels right to you. That could be as small as sharing an inspiring quote or book with someone or as big as starting a charity. Whatever it is, do it from your full heart, not out of a sense of obligation or attachment to a beneficial outcome.

Meditation for Gratitude

Preparation / About This Meditation

"The best way to get what you want is to love what you have." I have no idea to whom that quote belongs, but it's one of my favorites about gratitude and abundance. I found it shared as an inspirational meme on Instagram and saved it in my phone. It's a reminder for me to be grateful for what I have—especially if my desire is to have more.

It took a long time for me to be OK with wanting more. It took even longer for me to feel comfortable saying it. I was afraid of appearing greedy, and coming to terms with my desire for more required focused self-study . . . mostly through meditation.

My current life is one marked by abundance. I have all that I need and then some—a loving husband, healthy children, a job I love, and an incredible tribe of girlfriends who support and inspire me. I also have a lot of material comforts that I enjoy immensely. But yet, I want more—more love, more experiences, more introductions to interesting people . . . and, yes, more money, too.

Do you ever feel guilty about asking for more? In *The Law of Divine Compensation*, Marianne Williamson tells us that feeling guilty about our desire for more comes from a belief in lack. We believe that for us to have more, we have to take something away from someone else. This couldn't be less true. There is no lack in the Universe—only abundance. The Universe wants us to have more because having more allows us to give more. When we share what we have, everyone wins. The more we share, the more abundance is brought into existence.

The caveat to this is what I talked about before. Abundance doesn't just happen. Blessings from the Universe come easily, but you have to put the signal out that you're ready. You have to love what you already have to get more of it. Expressing gratitude signals abundance.

So, how do we demonstrate that we're ready for more? Writing in a daily gratitude journal is a way to remind yourself of your many blessings, but it's also important to send the message outward. You can do this during meditation.

When? My favorite times to practice this gratitude meditation are early in the morning and at night before bed. Beginning your day with gratitude will get you started on the right foot. Ending your day with gratitude prepares you for a restful night's sleep filled with pleasant dreams.

Where? Practice in your favorite meditation space or wherever you feel most comfortable. This is a light, joyful meditation, so you can feel safe practicing almost anywhere. Your Meditation for Gratitude could also serve as a midday pick-me-up if you need an extra jolt of energy or a quick confidence boost during the day.

Position? This is the first time I'm offering you Hero Pose, a pose that I feel perfectly complements the celebratory tone of this meditation. Refer to Chapter 2 for detailed instructions. You'll probably need a bolster, pillow, blanket, or bench to comfortably perform Hero Pose for the first time. Of course, if Hero Pose causes discomfort for you, you can use Easy Seat or Chair Meditation Pose instead.

Rest your hands on your thighs near your hip creases or on your knees with palms upturned.

Close your eyes if you're comfortable with it, and smile while repeating your mantras.

You Have 4 Minutes to Celebrate YOU

Sitting up tall in Hero Pose with shoulders back and your chest open wide, begin to ready yourself for 4 minutes of celebrating the miracle that is you. Surrender yourself completely to radical self-love. You deserve it!

1. Start by guiding your focus toward your breath.
   Follow your inhales and exhales as they fill and

empty your lungs. Examine closely how your breath is traveling in and out of your body. Notice how it feels passing in through your nose, past your nostrils, down your throat, and into your chest and belly. Allow your breath to settle in your seat. Feel it meet the surface beneath you. Follow your breath up and out again. Allow your jaw to relax as your breath passes your lips.

2. Now that you are familiar with the chakra centers in your body, visualize each chakra being lit up as your breath passes through it. Imagine the colorful glow of each chakra as it expands and grows brighter. Your breath—your life force energy—is like an energetic light switch turning on your chakras and creating a clear path for the wisdom, knowledge, and love of the Universe to travel through you.

    Your breath will carry your mantras to every part of your body, but especially up and down the core channel occupied by your seven main chakras. Notice the subtle energy shifts happening in your body as you repeat the mantras. You will notice yourself sitting taller and feeling lighter after each set of breaths.

    The following mantras are most effective when spoken out loud. Remember to smile, too! Let's make sure the Universe can't refuse its invitation to your self-love gratitude party.

3. Close your eyes and repeat each of the mantras below on the exhale for three breath cycles. Open your eyes after each set of breaths to read your next mantra. Remember to smile while repeating your mantras. This infuses each mantra with an extra touch of joy.

Mantra 1

I'm so happy, so healthy, and so blessed.

Mantra 2

I'm faithful in the little things. I'm grateful for what is.

Mantra 3

I have everything I need to be successful.
I'm ready to take on the world.

Express Gratitude for Your Practice . . .

4. Finish your meditation by taking three big breaths with your hands in Anjali Mudra (prayer hands) and your thumbs placed gently on your sternum (heart center). Fill your entire body with each inhale; let out a big, audible "ah" with each exhale.

5. You are energetically charged with feelings of gratitude. You're so blessed and so ready to receive even more abundant blessings. Take one last inhale. Then exhale and say, "Thank you, thank you, thank you," to seal your practice.

Meditation for Abundance

Preparation / About This Meditation

Let's talk about abundance and why living an abundant life supports doing good work on this earth. If you don't have enough food to eat, how can you feed someone else? If your bills aren't paid, where is the opportunity to be charitable? If you're overwhelmed with worry, what's left of you to offer to a stressed-out friend? Unless you have more than you need—money, time, and energy—how can you possibly share what you have with others? Abundance is a fundamental element of service. We need to *have* more to *give* more.

Once again, it's important to release guilt and the opinion that wanting more is about greed. It's the opposite of greed that attracts abundance. The Universe will always view *wanting more* for the purpose of *doing* and *giving more* as a noble desire. If our shared purpose in this life is to love and to be loved, to learn and to teach, the Universe will always show up in support of all our efforts to fulfill that purpose. The Universe wants to bless you with abundance because abundance leads to service. And service is the way we demonstrate God's love.

I've already got you covered with gratitude. You realize that you have a lot of reasons to be grateful. The Universe sees that you've been faithful in all things—big and small—and it wants to give you the responsibility of more. The Universe knows you're ready, I know you're ready, and now it's time for you to proclaim your readiness out loud.

When? Any time is the right time to welcome abundance. Start your day with your Meditation for Abundance, and allow the Universe to shower you with blessings from morning till night. Use this meditation at the beginning of any new project to wrap your venture in the cozy, loving kindness of a bountiful Universe. Practice at night to sprinkle your dreams with divine inspiration.

Where? I like to practice meditations and prayers for abundance in open spaces. An empty or uncluttered room allows space for new things—both energetically and physically. Practicing outside on an expansive lawn or open field takes this idea of open space to the next level and also physically connects you to the earth's vibration.

Position? You're going to use Hero Pose once again. Support your posture with appropriate props, or sit directly on the floor or ground if that's comfortable for you. I recommend practicing Hero Pose on a firm surface, whether or not you use props.

Place your hands on your thighs near your hip creases or on your knees with palms upturned in Kubera Mudra.

Open your eyes to read your instructions, and close them when guided, if you can.

You Have 4 Minutes to Welcome Blessings

You are grateful for what you have and receptive to more. The Universe wants to bless you with bounty because you're a kind and generous spirit. Sitting tall in Hero Pose, prepare yourself to welcome divine blessings.

1. Focus your attention on your breath as it is in this moment. Make no attempt to change it. Just acknowledge what a gift it is to be here now, blessed with health and vitality. Acknowledge how blessed you are to be breathing easily in this moment.

2. Close your eyes for just a few breath cycles and follow your breath's path through your body. Imagine your breath clearing space inside your body, sweeping away tension, unimportant thoughts, and any energetic clutter that isn't serving you right now.

3. Imagine the gentle glow of your Heart Chakra and Solar Plexus Chakra. Imagine their shining green and yellow lights expanding and contracting with your inhales and exhales. Imagine the glowing lights expanding outside your body and into the space around you. These lights will attract the attention of the Universe and will help you call forth abundance.

Signaling the Universe with Your Light . . .

Your chakras' glowing lights are attracting the attention of the Universe. They are sending a signal that is drawing abundance toward you. You feel energy pass through your heart center, fill your chest, and swirl in your belly. Gentle warmth radiates from your center outward, and your whole body feels warmed as it fills with energy.

4. Imagine the following message acting like an electrical current that turns your chakras' lights all the way up. The brighter the lights, the stronger the signal to the Universe. Read the following message two times either silently or aloud as you continue to visualize your glowing green and yellow lights: "When I think thoughts and speak words of abundance, the Universe provides me with all I need and more. I believe that what I already have is all I need for success, and this belief attracts kind and generous assistance. I know that I have all I need to be here now in peace and prosperity, and I will be rewarded with support in all my efforts for more."

5. Close your eyes and see yourself receiving abundant blessings from the Universe. See your lights return to their safe space inside your body, where they'll continue to be a container for your blessings long after your time in meditation is over. Once your lights are safe inside, open your eyes for your last step.

    Now you have a way to call on abundant blessings whenever you'd like. Just turn on your lights and make your desires known.

6. Bring your attention back to your natural inhales and exhales. Close your eyes and continue to breathe in silence for as long as it feels good. When you're ready, open your eyes to end your meditation.

Meditation for Service

Preparation / About This Meditation

Be faithful in the little things. Wait for abundance. Then, when your cup runneth over—and it absolutely will—say "thank you," and share. The sharing (or service) is the final ingredient in your magical recipe for manifesting wealth.

For the sake of this practice, "wealth" means anything that adds value to your life. Better relationships, more money, and a greater sense of self-love are all examples of wealth that are easily manifested through gratitude, abundance, and service. The formula is simple: gratitude invites abundance, and abundance inspires service.

The service part of the formula is particularly special because it's characterized by action. Acts of service that benefit others and the greater good are arguably the fastest way to affect big change in the world. Imagine the effect of lifting someone out of poverty, feeding someone who's starving, or offering kind words to someone who feels otherwise unloved. The act of being of service takes your practice off your pillow and into the world.

Then—once your practice is out in the world—something *super* cool happens. The service feels so good that your list of reasons to be grateful grows longer, blessings flow more abundantly, and you're provided with even more resources to allow you to be of service. The more you put the formula into practice, the more wealth is manifested. A simple routine that yields guaranteed exponential good results is created, and all it takes to maintain it is giving thanks, allowing blessings, and paying the blessings forward.

If what I just told you isn't motivation enough for going into the world and sharing whatever blessings you have, let me offer this meditation as further inspiration.

When? This is a meditation best practiced first thing in the morning before you set out into the world. Starting your day in a spirit of service creates a foundation for spreading love. Just your desire to be of service will attract positive energy from loved ones and strangers alike, and your generosity will be a magnet for the same.

Where? Practice your Meditation for Service in your personal meditation space. This practice should be regarded as a sacred expression of love, so save it for your most special spot.

Position? Sit in Easy Seat and place your hands on your thighs or knees with your palms upturned. For this meditation, your open hands represent the gesture of giving or offering.

Open and close your eyes when guided.

You Have 4 Minutes to Spread Love

This is your offering to your brothers and sisters on this planet. It can also be an offering to all living creatures and to the earth itself. Your gift of service can extend to everything that needs love and attention to thrive.

Service can manifest as a smile, a good deed, or a physical gift. The possibilities to be of service are endless.

1. Sitting up tall in your Easy Seat, allow your natural inhales and exhales to enter and exit your body freely and without manipulation. You feel physically and energetically light, and you're looking forward to your day.

2. Close your eyes and notice how your inhales and exhales are becoming smoother with every breath cycle. Focus all your attention on your breath for ten full breath cycles before opening your eyes to read your message.

3. Read your message aloud, slowly and quietly. Take a deep breath at the end of each sentence. Then read the next sentence on the exhale: "Today I will be a conduit for energy, joy, insight, and miracles. I'm

ready to share my gifts. There is enough for everyone, so I share willingly and with abundant love."

4. Close your eyes for three full breaths, and then open them again to read your final message in the same gentle voice: "I am a conduit for energy, joy, insight, and miracles. I share my gifts freely and with abundant love."

You Are a Vessel through Which Good Works Flow . . .

You've been strengthened by all the events of your life. You're a divine creation, capable of great things. You've been blessed with abundant gifts to share with the world. Sharing your gifts continues the magical, perpetual cycle of gratitude, abundance, and service that will bring you immeasurable wealth and happiness. Your purpose is clear. Go spread your light!

Chapter 12

MEDITATION IS YOURS

So, here we are at the end of this journey together. You made it through all 12 chapters, read a bunch of stories about my life, and practiced (at least most of) the 27 meditations.

You listened with an open heart, tried not to judge (even when what you read sounded a bit weird/silly/crazy), and actually put in the work of sitting down and getting quiet.

I made a promise to you at the beginning of this book that by the end you would be someone who meditates. You would no longer feel a separation between yourself and all those seemingly peaceful, calm, and spiritual people you've admired from afar—but couldn't relate to in the least.

I'm sure that even the title of this book was a promise that you were sure you'd prove false. In fact, you might be thinking right now, "Um, it doesn't look like my life has changed, and a lot more than four minutes has passed." You're not imagining things, but you're also wrong.

I'm going to be straight with you: I delivered on my promise and *more*. I not only proved to you that you do, in fact, have 4 minutes to change your life, but you actually *have* changed your life. If you've read this book and put into practice just a few bits of instruction that I've given you, you've done it. You came with an open mind and a receptive heart, fully dedicated to learning something new, and you took the first steps toward creating something wonderful—a meditation practice that you can carry with you for the rest of your days and years. You did it just by setting aside a few minutes to say hello to your inner self and show yourself a little love. That's awesome!

You now have a foundation to build a practice upon, and trust me—that really is life-changing!

Spread the Love

Even in stillness I am powerful movement, vibrant energy, and divine intention. And I'm a magnet for the same. #YH4M

Keep the Momentum Going!

Now, practice doesn't always mean perfect. You're looking around and thinking, "But everything looks *pretty much* the same." Maybe you've done some major unpacking (cleaning out that emotional closet) and stuff looks even worse!

If that's the case, it's cool. You're going to be OK. Really!

I get it, though. The spiritual evolution struggle is *so* real—*like, really real.* How many books do you have to read? How many lectures do you have to listen to? How many retreats do you have to attend after shelling out big bucks? When will you finally be enlightened . . . or at least make it through your day without feeling like you just went 12 rounds with Floyd Mayweather?

You want a big sign that things are all working out according to a perfect plan because, after all, you brought some pretty big effort to the table. But that big sign may never come. If you want evidence that things are working in your favor, all you have to do is keep showing up, honor your practice, and be disciplined in your good work. Detach from the results while doing your work, and the results will show up like you never thought they could— abundant, overflowing, and joyful.

Be faithful in the little things, and show gratitude for the tiny, but equally beautiful changes that you've been blessed with for your efforts.

Spread the Love

My wants are worthy. My voice has value. Practice creates proof.
#YH4M

But practice is the key! If you have a goal, go after it with consistent, dedicated, and forward motion. It's of no consequence whether the motion is short, long, big, or small. It's about moving forward in faith—sometimes even in fear—but always while doing your best to release attachment to the outcome. Those are the characteristics of a good practice.

The traditional goal of meditation was enlightenment. Don't freak out! We'll all get there . . . eventually. But the *practice* of meditation is what brings us daily peace, calm, contentment, perspective . . . and, yes, even joy.

Meditation saved me from drugs, anxiety, depression, self-abuse, and hopelessness. I meditate (and pray) daily, and I have to say that my life is pretty awesome. I'm off all drugs (even caffeine), my anxiety is easily managed, and I'm no longer depressed. I have tremendous confidence and self-respect, and I'm more excited about my future every day. I love myself so much!

Yes, meditation did all that. Again, there's nothing special about me that makes it work for me and not you, too. Each breath you take in meditation is an affirmation of your aliveness. It's a promise of a fresh start. It's proof that you've survived every struggle up until this moment.

Spread the Love

*I am fully supported in my efforts. I am free to
speak my truth in and to the Universe.* #YH4M

What we learn in our quiet times with ourselves—listening to our inner God wisdom—shapes our thoughts, words, and actions for all the hours of our days and follows us for the rest of our lives. Meditation is a practice of being a student and a teacher all at once. It opens us up to wisdom and a level of self-love that we never thought possible. It's a practice of deep connection, constant learning, inspired curiosity, and confident answering.

In order to thrive as human beings, we need to know that there's someone else out there just like us. We're not alone. We're fully supported, no matter what. Meditation, though practiced in solitude, allows for divine connection to Source, God, the Universe, the one pure energy that we're all connected to. It allows us to tap into the greater consciousness that beats our hearts and ignites our souls with dreams and desires. The time by ourselves on our meditation pillows allows us to also be in union with each other. Meditation removes the myth of separation and brings us back to the whole.

And now meditation belongs to you.

ACKNOWLEDGMENTS

Whatever words I could gather to express my gratitude for all who have encouraged, supported, and held me in my journey to bring my work out of my heart and into the world would be terribly inadequate. I feel beyond blessed for the friends, collaborators, and teachers God has sent me. For your loving support and inspiration, I extend my gratitude to Kris Carr, Ram Dass, Rachel DeAlto, Elizabeth DiAlto, Danielle Diamond, Sarah Dussault, Dr. Wayne W. Dyer, Molly Hahn, Alexandra Jamieson, Danny-J Johnson, Jessica Ortner, Michael Perrine, Yulady Saluti, Grace Smith, Tara Stiles, Erin Stutland, Quentin Vennie, and Heather Waxman.

This book project started out as something very different, and I'm so pleased by what it evolved into. That evolution wouldn't be possible without the help of my wise and caring literary agent, Wendy Sherman; my very patient and talented editor, Melanie Votaw; and my entire Hay House family, including Patty Gift, who gave me my first chance at this big dream. I thank you all for helping my thoughts become things.

Being loved is a purpose fulfilled. Thank you for loving me as is, Mom and Dad, Dani, Leah, and Aunt Kathy.

And for being my sun, my moon, my life, and my breath . . . for being my everything, I thank you, Justin, Winona, Calvin, Jack, Summer, and Annabel.

ABOUT THE AUTHOR

Rebekah "Bex" Borucki, founder of BEXLIFE® and the BLISSED IN® wellness movement, is a mother of five, TV host, meditation guide, author, speaker, birth doula, fitness and yoga instructor, and popular social media personality. She also travels extensively, sharing her love for yoga, wellness, and meditation at exclusive workshops, luxury retreats, and public events. Website: www.bexlife.com.

We hope you enjoyed this Hay House book. If you'd like to receive our online catalog featuring additional information on Hay House books and products, or if you'd like to find out more about the Hay Foundation, please contact:

Hay House, Inc., P.O. Box 5100, Carlsbad, CA 92018-5100
(760) 431-7695 or (800) 654-5126
(760) 431-6948 (fax) or (800) 650-5115 (fax)
www.hayhouse.com® • www.hayfoundation.org

❀

Published and distributed in Australia by: Hay House Australia Pty. Ltd.,
18/36 Ralph St., Alexandria NSW 2015
Phone: 612-9669-4299 • *Fax:* 612-9669-4144 • www.hayhouse.com.au

Published and distributed in the United Kingdom by: Hay House UK, Ltd.,
Astley House, 33 Notting Hill Gate, London W11 3JQ
Phone: 44-20-3675-2450 • *Fax:* 44-20-3675-2451 • www.hayhouse.co.uk

Published and distributed in the Republic of South Africa by: Hay House SA
(Pty), Ltd., P.O. Box 990, Witkoppen 2068
info@hayhouse.co.za • www.hayhouse.co.za

Published in India by: Hay House Publishers India,
Muskaan Complex, Plot No. 3, B-2, Vasant Kunj, New Delhi 110 070
Phone: 91-11-4176-1620 • *Fax:* 91-11-4176-1630 • www.hayhouse.co.in

Distributed in Canada by: Raincoast Books,
2440 Viking Way, Richmond, B.C. V6V 1N2
Phone: 1-800-663-5714 • *Fax:* 1-800-565-3770 • www.raincoast.com

❀

Take Your Soul on a Vacation

Visit www.HealYourLife.com® to regroup, recharge,
and reconnect with your own magnificence.
Featuring blogs, mind-body-spirit news, and
life-changing wisdom from Louise Hay and friends.

Visit www.HealYourLife.com today!